The Ramblings of the Man who Bought a Pear

JAMES WEBB

LIONESS
WRITING LIMITED

For Mark and Elsa.
When it comes to making me look good,
they've worked a lot harder than I have.

CONTENTS

JAMES WEBB

INTRODUCTION

Writing this blog started out as my contribution to publicity for *The Listening Book*. Elsa, the publisher, was working tirelessly behind the scenes to draw attention to my first book, while I was working tirelessly behind the scenes to avoid attention. Honestly, she deserves a medal.

A blog seemed like it would work for me. I had done one before after all, and I was supposed to be able to write. Blogging is also something of a private performance, like singing in the shower. You can be creative without it feeling like anyone sees or even cares about what you're doing.

I was doing some research on writing a blog...OK, I was reading some of the stuff Elsa had sent me that she had found when she was doing research on writing a blog, and one thing that stuck with me is that it had to be regular. In this day and age, if you can't be relied on to provide new content, people get bored and move on. So I decided that I would post something weekly, and it helped me to have my own deadline, so Thursday became blogpost day.

Writing a weekly blog is a little like skydiving. It looks easy, right up to the point where the ground is rushing towards your face at an incredible speed. Obviously, blogging leads to marginally fewer fatalities, but every week Thursday would seem to arrive earlier than it had last week and I would need an idea.

Some weeks it was easy. Some weeks it wasn't. But it was always good for me. I found out that I had more to say that I thought I did. I also discovered that it wasn't quite as private as singing in the shower, as I would get occasional posted comments and less occasional public comments, which would remind me that people were actually reading what I was posting.

A year has passed since I started the blog. The well hasn't run dry yet, though I always feel like it's about to. I'll keep going until it does.

Enjoy!

Third Time's the Charm...

24 October 2015

This will be the third blog that I have started. I began the first one soon after we moved to Australia and that was reflected in its content. It was very much 'An Englishman Abroad', with me attempting humourous observations on life Down Under like a third-rate Bill Bryson. I began the second blog years later as I attempted to discipline myself into writing on a regular basis. For a year and a half I posted a short story every two weeks, like a second-rate Stephen King. Much of that material found its way into *The Listening Book*, the imminent publication of which has been the catalyst for me fixing the punctures on my internet bike and setting out on this, my third blogging journey.

So let's see where we end up this time, as I share reflections on life, faith and stories, hopefully – this time – as a first-rate me.

JAMES WEBB

I Can't Sing, So I Have to Tell Stories

28 October 2015

'Of course, many of Maelwys' people had become followers of the Christ – especially since Dafyd's coming. But there were some with us who observed the old ways, so to make up for the missed revel, I played the harp and sang.

And it came to me while I was singing – watching the ring of faces around the night's fire, their eyes glinting like dark sparks, gazing raptly as the song kindled and took light in their souls – it came to me that the way to men's souls was through their hearts, not simply through their minds. As much as a man might be convinced in his mind, as long as his heart remained unchanged all persuasion would fail. The surest way to the heart is through song and story: a single tale of high and noble deeds spoke to men more forcefully than all of blessed Dafyd's homilies.

I do not know why this should be, but I believe it to be true. I have seen the humble folk crowd into the chapel in the wood to receive the mass. In all sincerity they kneel before the holy altar, mute, reverent, as they should be, but also uncomprehending.

Yet I have seen the eyes of their souls awaken when Dafyd reads out, "Listen, in a far country there lived a king who had two sons…"

Perhaps it is how we are made; perhaps words of truth reach us best through the heart, and stories and songs are the language of the heart.'

Merlin, Stephen Lawhead

Blessed are the Cynics, for they shall see God

30 October 2015

As a fully-paid up member of Generation X, my teenage years were full of angst and world-weariness. Even at my tender age, I was already wise to all the tricks of The Man and as discerning as any middle-class white kid from south Northamptonshire can be. When I became a Christian this cynicism transitioned quite nicely into my new faith, as it seemed to me that there were no shortage of fruitcakes and nutters in church leadership. Some of them shouldn't even have been let near heavy machinery, let alone given serious pastoral responsibility. Oh yes, I knew what was what. No-one would get one over me. My cynicism was so finely tuned that it was practically prophetic. I would watch my brothers and sisters work themselves up into a frenzy over the latest spiritual manifestation or teaching and I would remain calm, level-headed and quite unmoved. Unfortunately, cynicism can be quite indiscriminate at times, and I would still be unmoved even when it was God trying to do the moving. Thankfully I manage my cynicism much more responsibly these days. Some days it even borders on discernment.

At the end of the first chapter of John's gospel we find Philip excitedly relating to his brother that he's just met the Messiah, and Nathanael's response is so world-weary and sarcastic that I'm forced to conclude that he was actually British.

"Nazareth! Can anything good come from there?"

It's a classic response. Humourous and dismissive without actually addressing the issue. I recognise a fellow cynic when I see one.

The thing is, very rarely are people born cynical. Most of us spring forth into this world, wide-eyed and excited, hoping against hope for good things to come our way. But they don't, and cynicism is just one of many defence mechanisms that we evolve in order to protect ourselves. The secret is this, that many cynics are just disappointed idealists. We once believed, but were let down, and to avoid hurt we have chosen to never believe again. Thus another cynic is born.

In the years leading up to Jesus' birth there were Messiahs cropping up on a semi-regular basis. It was typical of the Israelites, chaffing under the unjust Roman yoke. Their freedom in the land was so bound up in their identity as God's chosen people that it should be no surprise that there were plenty of people willing to jump on whatever revolutionary bandwagon came along. Nathanael would, no doubt, have known about the one called Athronges. He claimed to be the Messiah and, get this, he was a shepherd. Many Jews would have just loved that Davidic parallel. The Romans took a dim view of such behaviour and, without fail, every Messianic pretender (Athronges included) would have ended up dead or imprisoned, along with his followers.

"Not another Messiah! Philip, why do you have to be so gullible? You're always falling for things like this…"

But if a cynic is just a disappointed idealist then maybe it's not Philip who's the gullible one? Maybe Nathanael's harsh reply is just his wounded heart talking? Maybe he once believed? Maybe it was once him, rushing into the desert after Simon, or Athronges, or some other deluded trickster, hoping that it would lead to the freedom that a true Israelite desired. Well, never again! Fool me once, shame on you, fool me twice, shame on me. But Philip is no fool himself. He knows that there's no point arguing or trying to persuade his brother. He gives the only reply that will work on a cynic:

"Come and see for yourself."

And Jesus sees him approaching. He appraises the young man. He smiles.

"Here is a true Israelite, in whom there is nothing false."

What a strange thing to say of a cynic. What is false if not Nathanael's bitter, dismissive reply to his brother? But maybe it's true. Maybe behind the sarcasm Jesus sees the heart of an optimist - one who dreams of what might be. A true believer.

"How do you know me?" Nathanael says, suspicion making him revert to type.

"I saw you while you were still under the fig-tree before Philip called you."

I don't see it myself, but there's obviously something in this phrase. Some secret that only God and Nathanael share. Whatever it is, it pushes all of Nathanael's buttons. He drops everything and gives such an overblown response that it would be funny if it weren't so perfect.

"Rabbi, you are the Son of God; you are the King of Israel."

From nought to sixty in under a second. It's almost as if he's been waiting for this moment his whole life. The cynicism, it seems, was just a mask to keep false prophets from the door while he was waiting for the real thing to come along. And here he is, coming from a place from where nothing good comes, and Nathanael is his, mind and soul. A cynic may no longer believe, but he still wants to.

"Jesus, I'm your man. For the rest of my life, I'm your man."

Here's the thing. While a cynic will keep everything and everyone at arm's length, if you can somehow break through his defences and give him a taste of the real thing he will flip-flop quicker than a politician. "Come and see for yourself."

Watch out for those cynics. They are not far from the Kingdom of God. A little taste of the real thing, and before you know it you've got a true believer whose passion will burn everyone and everything that they come into contact with.

"How Sharper than a Serpent's Tooth it is to have an Ungrateful Child!"

03 November 2015

Shakespeare must have had a thing about ingratitude. As well as contributing the title of this blog entry (it's from *King Lear*, fact fans), he also wrote the following:

> Blow, blow, thou winter wind.
> Thou are not so unkind
> As man's ingratitude.

That's from *As You Like It*. All I can say is that he must have been on the receiving end of some very insincere thank-you-for-my-birthday-gift letters. Mind you, he's a fine one to talk seeing as the only thing he left his wife upon his death was his 'second best bed'.

Many years ago there was a shipwreck off the coast of Evanston in Illinois. The students of nearby Northwestern University helped with the rescue operation. One particular student, Edward Spenser, personally saved the lives of 17 people that day. A long time later, when Spenser was an elderly man, a reporter asked him what was the one thing about that incident that stood out in his mind. Spenser replied, "I remember that of the seventeen people I rescued that day, not one of them ever thanked me."

Imagine that. A day in which you personally saved 17 lives and all you are left with is the memory of ingratitude. Blow, blow, thou winter wind indeed.

Nothing kills a gift quicker than ingratitude, and a lack of gratitude is a sure fire way to kill the gift of the Spirit of God. In Colossians 3:12 Paul is in the middle of spelling out how followers of Jesus, 'holy and dearly loved', should live. By the end of verse 17 Paul has instructed us three times to live gratefully. Three times in three verses actually. Thankfulness is a mark of being 'holy and dearly loved'. To be holy, we must put on gratitude.

But of course, God gives generously to those who don't deserve, holy and unholy alike. In Luke 6:35 Jesus reminds us that God is '…kind to the ungrateful and wicked', but I think it's rather telling that he lumps the 'ungrateful' in with the 'wicked', don't you?

The Thin Line Between Love & Hate

08 November 2015

I've just returned from speaking at our church on the topic of 'Love', because there's no reason why my first church-based speaking engagement in years should be about something, you know, *easy*.

I used to work for a charity called Tearfund. I was in the glamorous business of, as it was known back then, 'Income Processing'. That meant that if you sent in a donation, I was one of the people who made sure that your gift ended up allocated to the right project. You too can ascend to such dizzying heights if you have a degree in theology.

One day we received a letter with a donation. The gist of the letter was that the writer had been saving up to buy a new house, but that God had made it clear to her that she wasn't to move. The donation was, she wrote, the money that she had saved so far towards her new house. Her donation was a cheque for £80,000.

What I remember most about this was the letter. By the tone, the wording and reading between the lines I was certain that this letter should have had a postscript, and it should have read '*P.S. I'm not happy about this*'. There was a resigned frustration, a subtle anger in the wording. This was £80,000 worth of painful submission.

One day, an elderly man who had once walked around Palestine with an itinerant preacher and trouble-maker wrote his own letter, and in it you find the words, "This is love for God: To obey his commands."

What an intriguing paradox: the topsy-turvey Kingdom of God in action. Love for God has little to do with feelings, and much to do with obedience. Like the woman who surrendered £80,000, it is possible to be angry with God, resentful towards God, frustrated by Him, but if you do what He asks, then you love Him nonetheless. "A cold and broken Hallelujah," as Leonard Cohen sang. Hollywood tells us that we should have soaring violins and misty-eyed glances across a crowded room, but true love can be spitting bile as long as it obeys. After all, what you do shows to whom your heart really belongs.

In Which an Atheist Shows a Perfect Understanding of What it Means to Follow Jesus

10 November 2015

The entry for this week consisted of a quote from the Terry Pratchett book *Carpe Jugulum*. It's a passage that resonated with me, suggesting that those who take their faith seriously have an obligation to be more than just 'nice people'. We have chosen not to reprint the passage here because we're pending permission from the Terry Pratchett estate. In the meantime, feel free to go and look it up – *Carpe Jugulum*, ISBN 978-0552167611, pages 348 to 350.

JAMES WEBB

Peter & Paul

13 November 2015

I know a man called Paul. Some people might consider him eccentric, but I think it is much more accurate to understand him as being a perpetual whirlwind of creativity and kindness.

He once did something very silly, which was to metaphorically immerse himself (and his family) in the Gospel of Mark for a period of time. It was a silly thing to do because that's the kind of opportunity God might take to shift some heavy furniture in your life and, to be honest, who needs that kind of hassle?

Anyway, I imagine that he experienced all kinds of amazing revelations during this time, and he decided to share one of them with me. At least, I assume it occurred to him during this time. It might not have. It's possible he could have known it for twenty years and then randomly decided to drop it on me one day. As I said, he's a whirlwind of creativity and kindness.

In Mark 14, a woman anoints Jesus at Bethany. This fantastic little story appears in all four gospels, with particular nuances in each account. In Mark and

Matthew Jesus uses a strange little phrase that, I must admit, I'd never really understood: "I tell you the truth, wherever the gospel is preached throughout the world, what she has done will also be told, in memory of her."

I found it an odd comment. I suppose my confusion may have come from years of a particular type of Evangelical brainwas...I mean, teaching, where 'preaching the gospel' hadn't been done properly unless you had quoted a large chunk of Romans. Telling a story about some woman spilling a jar of oil over Jesus's head like a clumsy waitress didn't quite seem to cut the mustard. But Paul pointed out to me that, right here, Jesus links the telling of stories with 'preaching the gospel'. So, he said, perhaps, just perhaps, Jesus's expectation was that the main way that his disciples would share the gospel when he was gone was by telling stories.

Is Paul right? Well, I know another man. This one's called Pete. He's got the soul of a poet, and it's trapped in the body of a bouncer. Not really trapped, I suppose. It's more of a symbiotic relationship. Some people might consider him intimidating, but I think it is much more accurate...actually, OK, he can seem quite intimidating when you first meet him. But he's not really. Not when you get to know him, him and his gentle poet's soul.

He does silly things too, and as a result he's probably changed more lives for the better than he'll ever know. I heard that he once pointed out that when we want to evangelise we tend to mine Paul's letters for nuggets of theological truth, and forget that those same letters were actually written to people who were already Christians. If you want to share the gospel with non-Christians, he says, it's better to spend a bit of time looking at how it was done in the Gospels and Acts.

So if you look, what do you find? You find stories. Jesus tells parables, carefully encasing the whole Kingdom of God in each self-contained scrap of micro-fiction. That's a neat trick. In Acts, most of the recorded evangelistic speeches are just stories. Sometimes Paul shares his own story, but other times he, Peter and Stephen do nothing more than repeat people's own stories back to them, but each time adding a postscript: "Now let me tell you where Jesus fits into your story..." Indeed, it seems that when

Jesus was gone, the disciples preached the gospel by telling stories.

I am grateful for the things that these two men have shared with me. I am much more grateful for the two men themselves.

So, take note, men and women of faith! Do not neglect your story! Somewhere along the journey we may have lost our way, and belittled our stories. Do not do such a thing! Your story has been entrusted to you, and you alone, for the purpose of bringing the gospel of Jesus into the lives of family, friends, neighbours and curious strangers. Do not dare to be ashamed of it. Own it, and proclaim it, for when you do you are preaching the gospel.

Writers Wot Have Influenced Me - Part 1 of 4 Adrian Plass

19 November 2015

I hadn't been a Christian long before I fell in with bad company. And by that I mean that I started reading a lot of Adrian Plass. I read pretty much anything of his that I could get my hands on. I was a Plass junkie. I still consider *The Sacred Diary of Adrian Plass Aged 37 & ¾* to be one of the finest and most meaningful pieces of Christian humour ever written, while I still have fond memories of making my way through books like *Cabbages for the King*, *View From a Bouncy Castle*, *Clearing Away the Rubbish* and so on. When I was newly minted, starting to find my way and trying to avoid traps for young players, Plass's insights were invaluable. He is quite excellent at coming alongside his readers and offering meaningful encouragement to those who are struggling.

However, as I aged, the path that God had led me on meant that I often found myself up to my elbows in Other People's Problems, and – as some of you will know – that often has the amusing side-effect of bringing to the surface All Your Own Problems. I wanted to grow - to change. I didn't want to struggle through my faith the rest of my life thinking, "Is this really as good as it gets?" I needed solutions rather than sympathy, and as a result I seemed to find myself no longer in the audience that Adrian Plass was writing for.

Despite this, his impact on me in my needy youth was such that I am always interested when I hear that he has written a new book, and will probably automatically buy anything that has the *The Sacred Diary* name attached to it. Furthermore, there is a very specific piece of his that still influences my attempts at writing today.

As a teenager, I once got the opportunity to hear The Great Man Himself speak. I knew that he was available to sign books, so I bought what was probably the only Adrian Plass volume that I hadn't read at that time – a collection of short stories titled *The Final Boundary*. The actual encounter with The Great Man Himself was embarrassing, due to me briefly forgetting my own name, but I still have the faded paperback with 'To James, God Bless, Adrian Plass' written in the front.

What I like about *The Final Boundary* is that most of the stories avoid the thinly-veiled morality tale approach of a lot of Christian fiction. Plass is just happy to just dump a story in your lap and leave you to get on with it. I imagine that *Why it Was All Right to Kill Uncle Reginald* would have upset a few people in its time. *Marl Pit* still moves me. *The Second Pint* is perhaps the closest in style to one of Jesus's own parables, and by that I mean that it should leave the reader with chills running down his spine. Maybe it was this book of stories that first planted the seed that would one day blossom into *The Listening Book*, but even if it wasn't, I know that within is a tale that first opened my eyes to the possibilities of storytelling. It's a story called *Bethel*, about a snail who is being hunted by a sparrow, a fat child and a French chef. Without giving anything away, I will tell you that it's surreal, bordering on the absurd at times, and makes few concessions to the reader. After twenty years, I still can't say for certainty what message Plass was trying to communicate, and that excites me. Something different reveals itself each time I read, though from the very first time I knew that I was reading something special. It is this story that first allowed me to see that obscurity has value, that you can write something and trust God with its message. In that way, *Bethel* has influenced me; it taught me to write without fear.

Writers Wot Have Influenced Me - Part 2 of 4 Richard Wurmbrand

25 November 2015

In the early days of my faith I read *Tortured for Christ* by Richard Wurmbrand, a Romanian pastor who was imprisoned during the rule of Communism. The book left an impression on me and, in those early days, if I wasn't in a Christian bookshop browsing through the Adrian Plass books then I would have been in a Christian bookshop browsing through the Richard Wurmbrand books. His biographical account, *In God's Underground*, is absolutely fantastic. As Brian Clough might have said, "I wouldn't say that it's my favourite Christian autobiography, but it's in the top one."

One book that I read was *Alone with God*, which is a collection of his sermons. What makes them unusual is that they are sermons that Wurmbrand preached while he was in solitary confinement. As part of a routine to keep his sanity, he would preach a sermon in his cell every day, despite the fact that no-one was there to hear it. He says that he reduced their main points to rhyming couplets, and by doing so he was able to memorise the bulk of them. When he was released, one of the things that he did was write them down, and he claimed that he managed to recall 348 of the 350 that he had preached.

I find that feat of memory amazing enough, but when you consider that many of the sermons include extensive quotes from the Bible, Shakespeare and other sources, it becomes truly incredible. I can't help but think that the published articles were a lot more polished than the original sermons. Regardless, *Alone with God* was a very significant book for me when I was a younger Christian.

Many years later, while I was in Australia, I read a copy of the first collection of sermons that he wrote, the functionally-titled *Sermons in Solitary Confinement*. I'd found *Alone with God* to be insightful, powerful and influential. *Sermons in Solitary Confinement*. Blew. My. Mind. The sermons in this collection were raw and uncompromising in a way I'd never encountered before – these were the ones that read like sermons conceived in an oppressive hole deep in the Romanian earth. There is something incredibly unnerving about having a man bleed all over you, but you can't doubt for a second the strength and meaningfulness of his convictions. These sermons came from a dark place, but they blazed in a way that deeply challenged and comforted me, despite the distance of both years and geography.

One thing that had a large influence on both my writing and my personal walk was the book's introduction. Wurmbrand was obviously aware of the potential controversy of some of what he was writing so he warns the reader that he will find some disturbing and uncertain things within. This is not a place to find solid, consistent theology and doctrine, he warns, rather these are the outpourings of a soul in agony. But then he writes the following about those days: "I did not live on dogma then. Nobody can. The soul feeds on Christ, not on teachings about him." Wurmbrand survived his ordeal not because he knew a lot of theology, but because he knew Christ. Do you understand the difference? In that one line he put into words the yearning of my soul since the first day that I had bowed my head before my new master.

If there is one goal in my writings, it is this. I do not want people to learn about Christ through what I write. I want them to encounter Christ. There is a crucial and important difference, and I am thankful to Richard Wurmbrand for his writings over the years, in which he demonstrated that distinction. It has helped to make my faith real, rather than hypothetical.

Happy Black Friday!

27 November 2015

"Dad," said the child, "why is it called 'Black Friday'?"

Dad didn't even look up from his computer.

"What do you mean?"

"Well, why is today called 'Black Friday'?"

"I don't know," said Dad. "I suppose I could Google it."

"It's just that, well, 'Black Friday' makes it sound like a scary or sad or bad thing," said the child.

"Hmmmm…" said Dad, clicking on yet another banner that screamed BLACK FRIDAY SALE!!!!

"And it's not, is it, Dad?"

"No," said Dad, "it most certainly isn't scary or sad or bad. It's fantastic."

"Can we call it something else then, Dad? Something better?"

Dad stopped his browsing for a moment to scratch his chin.

"What, you mean something like 'Not Bad Friday'?"

"Something like that, but better," said the child.

Suddenly inspiration struck.

"Hey! How about 'Good Friday', Dad? Could we call it 'Good Friday'?"

Dad thought for a second. He couldn't think of a reason why not.

"Yes, OK. That seems like a much better name," he said, clicking on the button labelled 'BUY IT NOW'. "It certainly is a Good Friday! I've just got a great price on this camera!"

And that is how the tradition of Good Friday began.

Meanwhile, on an insignificant hill somewhere, a man died alone and in agony and no-one cared.

Writers Wot Have Influenced Me - Part 3 of 4 Fred Craddock

01 December 2015

I'm cheating a little bit here. Fred Craddock has influenced me not so much by what he has written, but rather by the way that he has said what he has said.

I hadn't heard of the diminutive American pastor until my preaching classes at Spurgeon's college, where we were exposed to one of his uniquely crafted sermons. For me, it was love at first sight…well, at first hearing anyway. He was, beyond doubt, one of the greatest preachers of the twentieth century, and many of you have probably never even heard of him.

There's a collection of his sermons (*The Cherry Log Sermons*), the style of which I slavishly attempted to emulate for my long-suffering congregation during my later years at Hayward's Heath, but it's the volume *Craddock Stories* that has shaped my own writing. The book is a collection of stories that Fred used in some of his sermons over the years, and they're fantastic. Not just the stories, but the way that they are told and the truth that is drawn from them.

Fantastic. He tells countless anecdotes from his rich life, but if he ever lacked a suitable story he would just make one up. I don't mean "Did I ever tell you about the time I had dinner with the Archbishop of Canterbury…" made-up, I mean a skilfully constructed parable of the imagination made-up . Let me give you an example:

I remember one night, sitting in a little rural church on a Sunday night. It was a summer meeting, so it was hot, and the window was open beside my pew. The minister was preaching on his favourite text, "Be not the first by whom the new is tried, because a bird in the hand is worth two in the bush, and it's better to be safe than sorry, because fools rush in where angels fear to tread."

I was listening to him drone away when a man came by the church building and stopped by the window and said, "Psst, psst."

I said, "What is it? I'm listening to the sermon."

He said, "Come with me."

I said, "Where are you going?"

He said, "I know where there is a pearl of great price that's more valuable than all the other pearls in the world."

I said, "There's no such thing."

He said, "In fact, where I'm going, there is treasure buried in a field."

I said, "You're kidding!"

He said, "Where I'm going, bums are invited to sit down at the king's table."

I said, "That's ridiculous."

He said, "In fact, they give great big parties for prodigals who come home."

I said, "That's stupid."

Well, I listened to the rest of the sermon and after it was over, I told the preacher about how I was disturbed and that I hoped it didn't upset him during the sermon.

He said, "Who was that?"

I said, "I don't know. Telling me all this fancy stuff."

He said, "Well, was he getting anybody?"

And I said, "Well, none of our crowd went, but I noticed he had about twelve with him."

I had never heard anything like this before, at least not in a sermon, and therein lies Craddock's influence on me. Stories make good sermon all by themselves but *imaginative* stories make *powerful* sermons. Let us try harder than to just pull out the same tired old illustrations that have been doing the preaching rounds since year one. Let us let our imaginations run rampant. Why should the devil have all the good flights of fancy?

Of the four writers that I am mentioning in this blog series, Craddock has had the most blatant impact on *The Listening Book*. There would probably be no book if it weren't for him. It contains more than one tale where I am self-consciously trying to ape his style of storytelling. Hopefully you won't be able to spot them! I'm finding my own voice now, but I don't want to ever forget the influence that Fred Craddock had on me.

Writers Wot Have Influenced Me - Part 4 of 4 Charles Williams

06 December 2015

Poor old Charles Williams. An amazingly talented scholar, poet and writer, and he gets no love just because he happened to be a lesser-known member of the Inklings and an Oxford contemporary of glory hogs C.S. Lewis and J.R.R. Tolkien.

I certainly hadn't heard of him myself, not until I moved to Australia and he was mentioned by a chap called Les Follent. Les talked about a series of, what he called, 'Christian Horror' novels that Williams had written. Well, my ears pricked up because the closest I had come to that genre was the *Left Behind* series, which I found horrific for all the wrong reasons. A few years later, when looking for a book to read, I got hold of the first of the six novels that he had written, *War in Heaven.*

Williams himself described the books as 'Spiritual Shockers', and they would probably be classified today as 'Supernatural Thrillers', though because they were written in the 1930s and 40s by an Oxford lecturer today's modern, desensitized natures may be tempted to turn their collective noses up at his work.

To be honest, his stories are best described as 'a mixed bag', but when he's good then he's *very* good. There are some brilliant high-concept plot ideas here. *War in Heaven* is about a rural parish priest who discovers that an old communion chalice that has been gathering dust in a cupboard in his church is actually the Holy Grail, and that a secretive practitioner of black magic is on its trail. That's an idea that's just waiting to be ruined by Hollywood. *The Greater Trumps* is about what happens when a selfish, manipulative Romany fortune-teller gets his hands on the original Tarot deck. *The Place of the Lion* is about what happens when a cult summons Platonic Forms into existence that begin draining reality from our world. That last one might sound a bit confusing, but if you have a basic grounding in philosophy then you might be thinking, "That sounds like the plot for the best film EVAR!!!"

Despite the sinister subject matter, each one is grounded in the assumption that God, and the cross, are the ultimate reality. Indeed, there's so much wisdom in the message of each book that you know that you are in the presence of a master. Williams avoids the gore and perversity-for-perversity's-sake that characterizes much of the genre these days, and injects subtle horror into his work. I remember reading a Stephen King comment about how the most terrifying horror is when the writer manages to twist the everyday aspects of life into something else - to turn the mundane into the malevolent. Williams manages this by capturing how our eternal character depends on those tiny daily decisions that we make; how tiny seeds of hate can eventually kill us; how little strands of lust or jealousy can grind down our souls until we cease to be human. Beware those mundane, everyday things! Indeed, *Descent into Hell* contains the finest temptation scene I have ever encountered, and demonstrates perfectly how our essence can hinge on the smallest of nails. This is the kind of truth that should chill and unsettle our modern, desensitized natures.

Williams has influenced me by showing that it can be possible to write intelligent Christian literature in all genres, and that it can be done in such a way that it can cross over into the mainstream. The truth speaks to everyone. If I ever attempt anything that approaches a 'Supernatural Thriller' then I guarantee you that it will be done with Charles Williams in mind.

A Song for Christmas

11 December 2015

For a long while my favourite Christmas carol was *Hark the Herald Angels Sing*. Apart from the rousing tune, I considered it to be one of the more theologically robust Christmas carols. That kind of thing has always been important to me, but I've mellowed a bit over the years. In the past I was so zealous that I even hesitated to sing the line 'Veiled in flesh the Godhead see...' because I thought that it flirted with the heresy of Docetism.

One song that didn't ever get a look in was *Little Drummer Boy*. Adding a child with a drum to the nativity story didn't seem to add anything, except bizarre anachronism and dubious collaborations between David Bowie and Bing Crosby. I could do without any of that.

A couple of years ago I was introduced to a version of the song that didn't suck (by a guy called Sean Quigley) and as a result I actually started reflecting on the words, which I'd never really listened to before. I began to realise that in many ways this was the most Christocentric of all Christmas songs.

While a lot of the thumping Christmas carols may have us declaring great (or possibly insipid and dubious) theological truths, *Little Drummer Boy* is a song about the personal response required by these truths. It's like the difference between a poem about the majesty of the ocean, and a poem about swimming in the sea. It has become especially poignant as I have seen my book edge its way towards publication. "Shall I write for you?" I say, and the baby Jesus nods. Like the little boy in the song, what I bring may seem paltry compared to other gifts that are laid before him, but, just like the little boy, the passion of my gift is what really matters. 'I write my best for him' and he smiles. He likes it when we make him smile.

The Man who Sold me a Pear

This post won the 2016 Good Samaritan short story award from the Association of Christian Writers in partnership with Street Pastors.

17 December 2015

We were in the supermarket to buy a pear for Imogen. She'd been asking for one all day, ever since she saw a picture of a pear in the morning and had been reminded that they existed. There were no pears at home, so I found myself in a supermarket, a single pear in my hand, queuing up to pay.

And I felt embarrassed.

It had been a tough six days, on top of a tough six weeks, which had come off the back of a tough six years. I was tired, and had been worn down by the harsh reality of living and moving and having my being in this tainted world. We had returned to the UK from Australia just under a year ago, and were gearing up for our fourth house move in as many months. I had been wearied by the dehumanising journey of simply trying to secure a place for my family to live. I had spoken to countless robotic voices, and a fair few human ones, giving and taking various details. I had been dragged through the mill, weighed on the scales and been found wanting; judged by our absence from the country and by our inadequate income. Whenever I described our situation I encountered awkward pauses, credit checks and patronising explanations as to why we needed to jump through a dozen impersonal hoops. After all that suspicion and contempt, my embarrassment made perfect sense.

You see, there I was, surrounded by shoppers with bulging trolleys and heaving baskets, holding one pear. Do you understand? We were wasting their time, me and my pear. Me, the less than human, offering something that was barely worth their while to sell. What would be the response of the worker at the till? Mockery? Contempt? "One pear? Couldn't you have at least bought two or three?" Would I even be worth any emotion? It's a difficult thing to find yourself in a place where the best that you can hope for is to be ignored.

I was called forward to a till. An older man, not old, but older than me, with a scattering of awkward teeth left in his mouth, like Stonehenge after an earthquake. I prepared myself for the worst.

"Just one pear today," I said, offering my feeble excuse to the God of the Till, hoping to stave off his wrath. If I make light of the situation perhaps I can escape with just a disdainful smile. I think I could handle that.

"Just one pear," he repeated, but there was no judgement there.

I handed him the fruit. It was duly processed.

"Fifty-four pence, sir," he said, without a trace of sarcasm.

Was that expensive for just one pear? I didn't care, because he called me 'sir'. Did you hear that? 'Sir'! Me, with my solitary Forelle pear! Surely I did not deserve a 'sir', not for fifty-four pence, but it was given anyway.

Emboldened by this kindness, I passed over a five pound note.

"Thank you, sir," he said, as though the tedium of having to count out four pounds and forty-six pence worth of change was a precious gift that I was passing on. How much effort would he have to expend for my pittance? How much of my fifty-four pence would make its way to his pocket? Surely none, and yet..."Thank you, sir,"

He passed over the handful of gold, silver and copper shrapnel. I received it as though I were receiving a communion wafer.

"There you go, sir. Would you like a bag?"

Nowadays you have to pay for the privilege of a bag, but not then. In those days, they were free. And he makes the offer. A *free* bag for my *one* pear! What generosity of spirit! What grace!

"No, thank you," I said, smiling as I passed the fruit straight on to my delighted daughter.

No bag, but the gesture meant more to me than a thousand bags.

"Have a good afternoon," I said. I meant it.

"You as well, sir," he replied. He meant it too.

I swear to you, in all seriousness, there were tears in my eyes as I walked from that till-bound saint and out of that supermarket. Until that moment, I hadn't realised just how bruised I was, and neither had I realised just how hungry I was for a little kindness.

"Come to me, all you who are weary and burdened," said Jesus, "and I will sell you a pear."

JAMES WEBB

Time for a Christmas Poem

23 December 2015

For no reason other than because it's Christmas, I'm going to post here one of my favourite Christmas poems, by a former Poet Laureate:

Christmas by John Betjeman

The bells of waiting Advent ring,
The Tortoise stove is lit again
And lamp-oil light across the night
Has caught the streaks of winter rain
In many a stained-glass window sheen
From Crimson Lake to Hookers Green.

The holly in the windy hedge
And round the Manor House the yew
Will soon be stripped to deck the ledge,
The altar, font and arch and pew,
So that the villagers can say
'The church looks nice' on Christmas Day.

Provincial Public Houses blaze,
Corporation tramcars clang,
On lighted tenements I gaze,
Where paper decorations hang,
And bunting in the red Town Hall
Says 'Merry Christmas to you all'.

And London shops on Christmas Eve
Are strung with silver bells and flowers
As hurrying clerks the City leave
To pigeon-haunted classic towers,
And marbled clouds go scudding by
The many-steepled London sky.

And girls in slacks remember Dad,
And oafish louts remember Mum,
And sleepless children's hearts are glad.
And Christmas-morning bells say 'Come!'
Even to shining ones who dwell
Safe in the Dorchester Hotel.

And is it true,
This most tremendous tale of all,
Seen in a stained-glass window's hue,
A Baby in an ox's stall ?
The Maker of the stars and sea
Become a Child on earth for me ?

And is it true ? For if it is,
No loving fingers tying strings
Around those tissued fripperies,
The sweet and silly Christmas things,
Bath salts and inexpensive scent
And hideous tie so kindly meant,

No love that in a family dwells,
No carolling in frosty air,
Nor all the steeple-shaking bells
Can with this single Truth compare –
That God was man in Palestine
And lives today in Bread and Wine.

JAMES WEBB

The Dark Side of Being Blessed

31 December 2015

The end of a year is a natural time to look back and count your blessings, right? Except sometimes I think that I'm not sure what is a blessing and what isn't. Sometimes I read these end-of-year letters that people send round and when they say, "God has blessed us in 2015" what they really mean is, "No-one had to go to hospital, the kids are doing well in school and we're a year closer to paying off the mortgage."

When Gabriel appeared to Mary he met her with the words, "Greetings, you who are highly favoured! The Lord is with you." In other words, he proclaims Mary to be blessed, but her response is to be 'greatly troubled'. When I was at university I had to read *Fear and Trembling* by the Danish philosopher Soren Kierkegaard. Kierkegaard makes the observation that after this meeting, Gabriel did not then pop next door to the neighbours and say, "Do not despise Mary, something extraordinary is happening to her." Instead Mary had to bear the stigma of pregnancy outside of marriage, and all the shame and misunderstanding that went with it. "Greetings, you who are highly favoured…" said the angel, and then he left. That is why Kierkegaard writes, 'And is it not also true here that the one whom God blesses he curses in the same breath?' Mary knew what was going on. Greatly troubled. She understood.

God is gracious to us in our needs and in our wants. Being well-fed and at peace is something to be thankful for, but do we understand that true blessing comes with pain, because true blessing is always about being used by God, furthering the Kingdom and becoming more like Christ? These things carry with them a sharp edge and a responsibility. This is what was in my mind when I wrote 'Gifts', a story that appears in *The Listening Book*. It is also, no doubt, what was in C.S. Lewis's mind when he wrote the following: 'We are not necessarily doubting that God will do the best for us; we are wondering how painful the best will turn out to be.'

Here's to a blessed 2016.

As Yet Untitled

07 January 2016

I read a book.
The author's search
for the Jesus of our church.
"It turns out, as you can see,
that Jesus was just like me:
A Liberal, Western-educated, postmodern, hipster,
beardy social justice warrior."

I read a book.
The author's search
for the Jesus of our church.
"It turns out, as you can see,
that Jesus was just like me:
A middle-aged Conservative white American male,
angry at gays, Muslims, the unemployed and Russia."

I read a book.
The author's search
for the Jesus of our church.
"It turns out, as you can see,
that Jesus was just like me:
A bland, cringing, spineless academic who just wants
everyone to be happy and is trying desperately to
avoid giving offence."

I read a book.
The author's search
for the Jesus of our church.
"It turns out, as you can see,
that Jesus was just like me:
A black, bisexual, left-handed Wiccan who cares
deeply about animals, making wicker baskets and
bathing in her own urine."

But where am I to begin
if I just want to be like him?

Walking with God

15 January 2016

There are many reasons why I like to go for a walk, but two of them are as follows:

a) I like to get away from people every now and then.
b) I like to spend time with God.

However, those two reasons are not mutually exclusive, which is a common mistake we introverts often make. Another mistake is to assume that during those lonely strolls the only thing God wants to do with us is internal. Those of us prone to mysticism can be so lost in our thoughts that the rich young ruler could come to us and say, "What must I do to be saved?" and our instinctive response would be, "Push off, I'm praying."

The thing is, when you try to get away in order to spend time with God, you're climbing into the ring with Him, and sometimes He fights dirty. You just want a bit of peace and quiet in order to reflect and have Him all to yourself, but He just can't help trying to draw your attention to the universe outside. If you really want to spend time with God, you have to take the rough with the smooth. Thankfully, I've had some excellent teachers, so now I tend to go for my prayer walks with one eye on my soul and the other on the world around me.

Richard Wurmbrand tells of the first time that he ever entered a church. As an eight-year old he went in with a school friend who had been sent to deliver a message to the Catholic priest. After the message had been passed on, the priest spoke to Richard.

"What can I do for you, little fellow?"

"Nothing. I just entered with my friend," said Richard.

"I am the disciple of One who has taught me never to allow anybody to pass near me without doing him at least a little bit of good. It is hot outside. Would you allow me to bring you a cup of cold water?" said the priest.

Wurmbrand said it was the best cup of water he'd ever tasted.

That's pretty good. I would like it if the word 'Christian' was synonymous with 'One who never allows anybody to pass nearby without doing at least a little bit of good'. I try to keep that in mind when I'm out and about, because God's always at work. If I'm trying to hang out with Him then I should expect to be dragged into such things.

God Bless Restrictions

21 January 2016

One piece of advice that artistic people often give is that restrictions and constraints are good for creativity. I've heard this from artists, writers, film makers and computer game programmers, so it must be true.

Actually, it is.

If you give an artist a blank piece of canvas then what is he supposed to do with it? If you tell him that you want a picture of a tree, well, it doesn't require much in the way of creative thinking but at least it's something. If you tell him that you want a picture of a tree, and that it can only be in black and white, and that if you turn it upside down it must then look like a picture of a little girl – well, now you're talking. That's when the creative muscles get a workout.

I've dabbled in Microfiction (aka Flash Fiction), which for those of you who don't know, is a discipline where you subject yourself to an arbitrary word count (usually well under a thousand words) and set yourself the task of writing a complete, coherent story. I've found it a highly useful exercise, especially as my stumbling attempts to transfer my fleeting philosophical musings from the centre of my thought processes onto a sheet of blank paper have a disarming habit of running to the verbose. You know what I mean.

I'm currently working on editing a batch of stories for the sequel to *The Listening Book*, and a couple of those were born from constraints. When I was describing *The Listening Book* to a friend he asked me if one of the stories was called 'The Parable of the Boy who Ran with Scissors'. Trust me, this is fairly typical of the type of question that he asks. I replied that there was not, but the very next day I sat down and set myself the task of writing a story with that exact title. I'm quite pleased with it.

Perhaps that's the way I should go. I could get other people to suggest titles, and then I have to write a story to attach to them. So, if you have any imaginative titles lying around feel free to throw them in my direction, and if I'm looking for a challenge one day I could try writing a short story for it. Maybe I'll post it here, maybe I won't. It depends on whether or not it'll make me look creative.

The Myth of Good Stewardship

28 January 2016

P aul writes a few things about giving money. He tells us to be generous, to be cheerful, to give as God has given to us, but he never tells us to be shrewd with what we give. And yet, some of us treat our financial giving like we might treat a stock portfolio.

"I must get the biggest bang for my buck. I must make a good investment, and get the biggest return I can on my money…"

I'm sure, somewhere, that there's a man who has compiled a spreadsheet, where he is comparing various good causes and working out the 'Souls Won per Dollar' ratio. I imagine that he also thinks that God is likely to give him a pat on the back at the end of the day, but I wonder if instead God might aim a bit lower down and use His foot.

Like everything else, our giving must be submitted to God's agenda. And by God's agenda, I don't mean 'what we assume God's agenda is'. You don't arrive at God's agenda by dividing Middle Class Values by the Protestant Work Ethic. You arrive at

God's agenda by seeking, praying, fasting and listening.

Have you ever given to someone who is needy through their own sin and short-sighted mismanagement? Have you ever given to someone even though you know that there's a better than even chance that they'll waste or misuse your gift? Have you ever given to someone who has taken advantage of your generosity once already, and is coming to you a second time cap in hand? God has, and does every single day. And I'm not just talking about salvation, I'm talking about every aspect of His providence. I'm talking about how he gives to *you and me*. We are called to give as God does, and yet I know that some of us break out into a cold sweat at the thought of such irresponsible generosity. Yet, good stewardship is not about using your resources according to the values of Middle Britain. Good stewardship is about using your resources to the best of your ability according to the call that God places on your life. You give as He gives to you, whatever that may look like, and leave the rest to Him. I'm not talking about being stupid or irresponsible, I'm talking about being obedient and about not being self-righteous enough to assume that God only wants to give to the people that you think deserve it.

Fred Craddock once preached on the parable of the Prodigal Son, and was approached afterwards by a member of the congregation who happened to be a lawyer. He proceeded to tell Fred that he didn't like that particular parable.

"What is it you don't like about it?" said Fred.

"It's not morally responsible," he said.

"What do you mean by that?"

"Forgiving that boy," said the lawyer.

"Well, what would you have done?" said Fred.

"I think when he came home he should have been arrested."

"What would you have given the prodigal?" said Fred.

"Six years."

JAMES WEBB

A Lesson in Humility

04 February 2016

Whoen it comes to me, most worship leaders are up against it from the start. I have no musical talent myself, and therefore little appreciation of the skill required to play the handful of chords that most worship songs seem to employ. Neither am I a big fan of the contemporary worship style – on the whole, I like my music to have a little more edge. Furthermore, I've suffered over six years of formal theological training, so find myself hyper-critical of and disappointed by the content of most lyrics. Finally, many more years of hard yards in following Jesus, and trying to help others to follow Jesus, has resulted in me having nothing but contempt for the shallow, I-feel-pretty-good-about-God-right-now sentiment of many worship songs.

However, whenever I find myself drifting too far down the path of seething rage, I remember what C.S. Lewis said. He too struggled with the church music of his time, considering it fifth-rate poetry set to sixth-rate music, but he also wrote, "I realised that the hymns (which were just sixth-rate music) were, nevertheless, being sung with devotion and benefit by an old saint in elastic-side boots in the opposite pew, and then you realise that you aren't fit to clean those boots. It gets you out of your solitary conceit."

Hard as it is to believe sometimes, not everything is about me.

Giving God Room to Speak

11 February 2016

When I set aside time to spend with God, I make a habit of trying to spend some of that time listening. This can take many forms. Sometimes it'll be about what I'm reading, or what has been happening in life, but often I will have a time of silence where I wait on God and see if the Holy Spirit has something to say.

When I was the dean at Cornerstone Canowindra I would get phone calls from people who were interested in coming to spend a year studying and working with us. Sometimes, as the person told you their story, you would get a clear feeling that them coming wasn't going to be a good thing for them or for the community. But, if I could, I would avoid saying "No" right there and then. My preferred option was to explain to them what my concerns were, and then suggest to them that I have a few days to think and pray about it, before getting back to them with my final recommendation. After all, it's in your own interest to give God the opportunity to let you know if you're about to make a mistake.

The Listening Book has this thinking at its heart. It's really nothing more than a tool to help you slow down and give God some space to speak. You don't need it – there are plenty of ways to do that – but it's an important idea to me, and I thought that it wouldn't hurt to have a book about it. I know that when I talk about 'hearing God speak' there are all kinds of things (and warning bells) that can go through people's minds, but I am convinced that we don't really expect God to speak to us, so we don't even give Him a chance, and so it's no wonder that we never hear anything.

Indifference

18 February 2016

When Jesus came to Golgotha, they hanged Him on a tree,
They drove great nails through hands and feet, and made a Calvary;
They crowned Him with a crown of thorns, red were His wounds and deep,
For those were crude and cruel days, and human flesh was cheap.

When Jesus came to Birmingham, they simply passed Him by.
They would not hurt a hair of Him, they only let Him die;
For men had grown more tender, and they would not give Him pain,
They only just passed down the street, and left Him in the rain.

Still Jesus cried, 'Forgive them, for they know not what they do,
'And still it rained the winter rain that drenched Him through and through;
The crowds went home and left the streets without a soul to see,
And Jesus crouched against a wall, and cried for Calvary.

G. A. Studdert-Kennedy

JAMES WEBB

The Parable of the Talents - One

25 February 2016

Ah, Matthew 25:14-30. 'The Parable of the Talents' practically writes its own sermon. "So, in conclusion, God wants us to use our gifts for Him. Coincidentally, we need people to help lead the Sunday School. There's a sign-up sheet at the back." I did mention that I'm cynical, right?

I remember sitting in a classroom, waiting for the lecturer to arrive. He came in and, out of the blue, went off on a rant that had nothing to do with the session that was scheduled. "Some of you," he said, "are frustrating God because you're not using your gifts". Having delivered this message, he calmed down and got on with the lecture that we were supposed to have. I suspect that, years later, he wouldn't even remember that he'd done this and I'm certain that he has no idea that he was talking to me. Make no mistake, he was talking to me. That random little outburst changed my life. There would be no *The Listening Book* if he hadn't been obedient enough to vent on the Holy Spirit's behalf.

If Jesus had wanted the message of this parable to be 'God wants you to use your gifts' then he probably would have finished at verse 25, but he didn't. Verses 26 to 30 bring the story to its chilling conclusion. The servant who buried the money loses the little that he was entrusted with and is thrown into the sinister 'Outer Darkness'. No wonder we don't dwell on that bit. After all, you can understand why the servant did what he did, right? Would a little empathy have killed the master? And before you check, Luke's version isn't much better.

These days, when I read this parable I think about the times that I diligently prepared sermons, carefully making the message of Jesus a little more palatable for my congregation. Perhaps it was because I'm a sensitive, pastoral soul, or maybe it was because I was labouring under the mistaken belief that you can make a rose more beautiful by removing its thorns. These days I am even more committed to taking responsibility for how I am communicating, but I am equally aware that I am not doing God some great favour by coming up with eloquent and clever ways to de-fang the Gospel.

What if Jesus's message here isn't 'God wants you to use your gifts', but rather that 'Waste makes God angry'?

If that's true, what do you make of that?

JAMES WEBB

The Parable of the Talents - Two

03 March 2016

My family and I were part of Cornerstone Community for about eight years. For those of you who don't know, Cornerstone is an Australian mission and discipling movement, and it's been going for about as long as I've been alive. It's far from perfect, but it must have been doing something right. There are countless well-meaning Christian communities that have imploded within their first five years. Why has God kept Cornerstone around? What is the magic ingredient?

I wonder if one of the things that God enjoys about Cornerstone is that, fundamentally, it's a risk-taking venture. I'm sure those who are responsible for the organisation's accounts will agree with me, but others might not be so sure. Well, trust me. I've been involved in local church leadership and been a member of the Baptist Union of Great Britain, so I know what I'm talking about – There are churches that consider themselves 'edgy' because they've recently changed the time of their evening service. There has always been a touch of the Mad Scientist about Cornerstone – "Well, if Jesus really said *that*, what happens if we try *this..*?" I think God likes it. I'm not sure there's a risk-free way to build bridges to heaven.

There's a lot of theology you can be wrong about, and still be a Christian. Predestination, women in leadership, the Rapture, what worship really is, the role of Israel in God's plans, what the point of the Sabbath is, whether or not Donald Trump is the Antichrist etc. I used to think that my position on some of those things was really important. Now I'm not so sure. However, I do know that there are plenty of churches where the stuff about Jesus being God and dying for our sins and all that is just a given, and that the real meat and drink is in the kind of stuff that I've just listed – and you'd better make sure that you believe the right things. I know of at least one church where ministers are selected based on their response to a grilling from the congregation about these kind of issues (maybe not the Donald Trump one).

The thing is, what happens if you subconsciously create a church environment where it's a terrible crime to believe the wrong thing about these topics? What if everyone has to be on the same page about everything, or they're *persona non grata*? What if what you've communicated over the years is not actually the gospel, but rather the message that the worst sin in the world is to get it wrong? What happens to a church like that? It won't be a risk-taking church, because the problem with risks is that sometimes you can get it very wrong.

I remember taking a very specific risk once, and it going wrong. I crashed and burned in a humiliating way. The scars from that failure are still with me – all these years later and I still haven't totally recovered. But I don't regret it for a second, because I know that if God ever brings it up in conversation I can say, "Sure God, it didn't work out brilliantly, but at least I tried." I'm sure that God's response will be to smile, because He is a risk-taking God and has a soft spot for risk-taking children. I remember hearing a story once about a woman who criticised D.L. Moody for the way that he evangelised. His response: "I like my way of doing it better than your way of not doing it." I think that God agrees.

When I read 'The Parable of the Talents' another thought that I can't get out of my head is that there are no rewards, no prizes in heaven for caution. Quite the opposite, in fact. Sometimes, as I read it, I wonder what the master's response would have been if the servant with five talents had lost them all in his investment scheme. I like to think that he would still have had more time for that servant than for the one who sat on his hands. I don't know for sure, and such speculation doesn't really have a place in the interpretation of parables anyway. Jesus told it to make a specific point, and a different point would have required a different parable altogether. Maybe if he'd been surrounded by reckless, careless disciples he would have told a parable about a man who suffered because of a foolish risk, but as it is he told a parable about a man who was rejected by his master because he was too cautious and not risk-taking enough. I wonder why he felt the need to tell us that one?

Seeing is Believing

10 March 2016

Sometimes seeing isn't believing. There will be people that look successful and content, but aren't. There will be marriages that look happy, but aren't. There will be people who look as though they are faithful and enjoying a close relationship with God, but aren't. Your eyes can deceive you.

At times, though, we deceive ourselves, and maybe what other people see is the truth. I'm thinking primarily about how faithful or not we imagine God to have been to us. Sometimes we wonder if He is keeping His end of the bargain, if He's providing for us or if He is with us in our troubles. Does He even care for us at all?

So here's my challenge. We know how it looks to us and how we feel about it, but how does it look to other people? Take a step outside of yourself for a moment. When other people look at you and your life, will they say that God is providing and caring for you just fine? God does do His part, and other people can sometimes see that better than we see it ourselves. I suspect that much of our uncertainty is because what we're really thinking is, "God isn't doing things the way that I want Him to do them." It's like that old truism – most people are very happy to serve God, but only in an advisory capacity. So, being objective for a second, stop thinking about how it feels to you and ask yourself what it looks like to other people?

Origin Story

17 March 2016

It's nearly a year ago that Lioness Publishing first agreed to take on *The Listening Book*, but it's been in the pipeline for a lot longer, obviously. The oldest story in the collection (*Death*) was written over fifteen years ago, while even the most recent stories only exist because those past fifteen years gave me something worth writing about.

A couple of posts ago I shared a watershed moment, the one where I was challenged to actually do something with the gift that God had given me. This was way back in 2007, and I responded by resuming an Interactive Fiction project that I had shelved. *A Fine Day for Reaping* went on to win the XYZZY Award for Best Story in 2007. That sentence will make no sense to most of you.

Around the same time, however, I also began playing with parables. I was working for 'The Mat Exchange', which was a small business that Cornerstone ran. We rented door mats to shops, and my job was to drive around, exchange the dirty mats for clean ones and then go and wash them. There was a reasonable amount of time to think in this job and, one day, I was reflecting on the idea of faith, and how often I met people with an 'inherited' creed, beliefs that they'd just copied from others, without thinking through the consequences or really owning them themselves. I had previously read about the idea of how photocopying a photocopy decreased the quality of the image, and that had stuck with me over the years. As I drove along the mean streets of Dubbo, New South Wales, Australia, *The Soul Painting* was born, and by the time I had finished my shift that day I was able to sit down and write the story. Over the next few months I wrote a couple more, including *Knock and the Door Shall be Opened*, and *By the Riverbank* but I didn't really do anything with them.

Fast forward to 2013. Now I was dean of the Cornerstone campus at Canowindra. No more mat washing for me! Instead I got to do farm and vineyard work. There can be some thinking time there too, at least when you're not being shouted at. One day, while picking watermelons, I thought that it would do me good to set myself a challenge. The challenge would be to start a blog, and post a short story every week. At first this worked fine, as I was finally able to use the stories that I had accumulated over the years. The real goal, however, was to force myself to come up with new material, and that's what I did. Watermelon time was occasionally fruitful (pun intended). I remember concocting *The Boy who Held God* during one beautiful sunny day while picking watermelons (to be fair, it was almost always a beautiful sunny day during watermelon season). I soon found that one a week was an unrealistic pace, so I knocked it back to one every two weeks and just got on with it. When you write under pressure like that what you produce could charitably be called 'a mixed bag'. Some of the stuff that I put up was fairly horrible, but all of the material that ended up in *The Listening Book* first appeared on my blog: 'Storycatcher' ("Don't look for it; it's not there anymore." – Marty DiBergi).

The feedback was encouraging, so in the months before we returned to the UK, I put together the first draft of *The Listening Book* and sent it off to a publisher, who promptly rejected it. Well, not promptly. It took him ages. And then that was that, until we returned home and a random conversation between Elsa the Publisher and my wife started the ball rolling. I like to think of it as a large, heavy glittery ball – something nice to look at, but with some weight to it. Perhaps a disco ball that's been made out of concrete?

And the rest is, as they say, history.

The Discipline of Smiling

24 March 2016

I don't want them. My spirits are not lifted to see them; my heart is hard and cold. The visitor at the door is an intruder, wanting to take from me.

So what do I do? What I want to do is communicate to them, in a non-verbal way, that they are not welcome. A scowl. Closed body posture. An irritated tone. All these say "Go Away!" without me actually having to speak the words out loud. It's not a sin that way, right?

And why not? I am busy. I am in the middle of something, and there's a fifty percent chance it could be something quite important. I don't have much time in the day. I don't have much of myself to spread around. Besides, I'm an introvert. All the blessings that being an introvert bring come at a price to somebody else, and really, I think that they should consider themselves honoured to pay that price.

Weary and unbending, I want them to go away.

But that is not an option. I can't do that. I know this. I have a Bible. I know all the things that Paul says about loving one another and bearing each other's burdens and all that, but those aren't the words that break me. What does it is that wonderful, horrible story in Matthew 14 where Jesus withdraws to grieve over the death of John the Baptist. He just wants a moment to himself. A moment to be with his Father and his thoughts. You understand that, surely. I understand it. I live it.

But the stupid, selfish crowd can't see beyond their ugly sense of entitlement and their greed and they follow him. They won't leave him alone, not even for a second. Like everyone, they want a piece of him. They want to be made whole, but their stupid, selfish vision won't allow them to see what it costs Jesus. They can't see beyond themselves. Self-centred. Self-focused. Stupid, selfish crowd.

But then…Jesus gets off the boat and sees them. What happens to the God-man? What stirs in his soul? Anger? Pain? Bitterness? No. I'll tell you what it says.

"…he had compassion on them, and healed their sick."

Give me a pair of scissors and I will cut that verse from my Bible and yours. I would expunge all record of that moment of compassion from history. Do you not see? Do you not understand? Those words will not leave me alone. I cannot sleep. I cannot get peace. He had compassion while I was angry. He breaks the power of darkness while I send away. So, now you understand why I cannot allow the same thing that drove the crowd to drive me. Now you know why I cannot send them away.

So I submit myself to the discipline of smiling. When they come, I will smile. I may not feel compassion, but I can smile. I may not heal their sickness, but I can smile. I can deny the anger, the resentment and the bile that stirs in my soul and I can smile. I know enough to know that this is how it begins. The smile is the start. I know that one day, if I live this discipline enough, I will look up and see the face at my door and the smile will already be there before I even have to think about it. And I know that another day will come, a day when I will see the face at my door and I will *feel* like smiling, no matter what urgent task consumes me. I will become my smile.

I can hear the voice now. Liar! No Integrity! No Authenticity! By smiling when you resent you are denying the truth.

And I know where that voice comes from. I know well, and I rebuke it. He is the liar. His is the call to no authenticity and no integrity.

Listen. John says it best – "How marvellous is the love that the Father extends to us. Just look at it – we are called children of God. And that is what we really are."

And that is what we really are! So, if that is who I really am, then which action is the one that lacks integrity? The smile or the frown? If who I really am is a child of God, then it's the anger and the resentment that doesn't belong. It's *that* which is at odds with who I really am. The feelings are the lie. The smile is the truth breaking through. The smile is just me being who God has made me. The rest of me just hasn't quite caught up yet.

So, If you appear at my door and I do not seem pleased to see you, do tell me. I am trying to follow the discipline of smiling.

Mixed Messages

30 March 2016

It's hard to be a consistent parent, but you'd think we'd at least give ourselves a fighting chance.

I once saw a mother laying down the law to her little boy, her tone of voice suggesting that disobedience would have serious consequences. She had clearly had this type of conversation before. As she delivered some very specific instructions on behaviour, backed up by the existential threat of 'grounding', I couldn't help but notice her tee-shirt. It was plain, except for the big pink letters on it that read 'BREAK THE RULES'.

Hmmmmmm...

Tolstoy's Greedy Farmer

07 April 2016

There's a story by Leo Tolstoy about a peasant farmer who had done well in life, but wanted more. One day someone made him an offer. For 1000 Roubles the farmer could have as much land as he wanted, provided that he was able to walk around it in a day. The only condition of the deal was that he must be back where he started from by the time that the sun set.

Of course, he set out early the next morning moving as quickly as he could. At midday he decided that he would keep walking, and simply make sure that he moved faster on his return journey. By mid-afternoon he had walked a great distance, but he realised that he would lose it all if he didn't get back and that he hadn't left himself much time. He retraced his steps, running and running, trying to return to the starting line before the sun went down.

Just as the sun was beginning to dip below the horizon he came within sight of where he had started, so he pushed himself for the final few minutes, despite his complaining body. He staggered across the line, just as the sun set, and then promptly collapsed and died of exhaustion.

His servants dug him a grave, about six feet long by three feet wide. Tolstoy called his story 'How Much Land Does a Man Need?'

For Sale

14 April 2016

I've written briefly about the concept of Christian horror in my blog on Charles Williams and I've also mentioned my dalliance with Microfiction. The two intersect on a website that I occasionally contributed to – *MicroHorror*.

MicroHorror is now no longer live, and I hadn't written anything for it in nearly four years, but buried on there is my one attempt to communicate something meaningful through horror. It's a mere 200 words, and it's called 'For Sale'.

———

Come... on... MOVE... you... son... of... a...

Muscles bulged but the jar lid remained unrepentant. This was getting embarrassing. It had seemed like such a good idea at the time, such a simple idea. Offer to open the new jar for the girl in the kitchen. Impress the girl of his dreams. She didn't look impressed right now. She looked bored.

I... can't... believe... this... is... happening...

Still no movement. Not even a fraction of a fraction. The girl had stopped looking bored and was now beginning to look faintly amused. He didn't know which was worse.

She's... laughing... at... me... please... open... please... I'll... do... anything...

Suddenly a hissing, slithering voice whispered in the silence, in the deepest backdrop of his mind.

"Anything?"

***

In the darkness of the under realm, the two demons put the finishing touches to the contract.

"...for the ability to open a jar of sun-dried tomatoes? *Really?*"

The first demon sounded shocked and a little disgusted. The second demon nodded dolefully.

"There's no challenge these days. It's just not fun anymore," he moaned.

The first demon finished the document with a flourish of his pen, and slowly shook his head.

"You know what I reckon? I reckon those humans have stopped taking their souls seriously."

I Am Not a Christian

21 April 2016

They call me a Christian.

I am not a Christian.

They tell me that I am a Christian and that I should not be ashamed to be a Christian.

I ask them what it means to be a Christian.

They tell me that a Christian is one who has, at one point in their life, asked God to forgive his sins; One who has asked Jesus into his life.

If that is all it means then I am not a Christian.

A single "Yes" may make a Christian, but it cannot make a disciple. A man may be a Christian if he bows his head to Jesus once in his life, but a man can only be a disciple if he bows his head to Jesus every day.

I am not a Christian.

Call me a follower of Christ, one who hopes to walk so closely behind that he is covered in the dust that is thrown up as his master walks.

Call me a slave to righteousness, one who has relinquished all rights to himself but instead allows Jesus to live through him.

Call me a joint-heir with Christ, one who inherits what was not his, and seeks nothing more than to announce his brother's kingdom to the world.

Call me free indeed, and one for whom it is no hardship to submit that freedom to Him who makes me free.

Call me a New Creation, God's Workmanship, a Living Stone, a Holy People, a Saint, a Son of the Living God.

But do not call me a Christian.

A Preaching Odyssey

28 April 2016

The only thing that I miss from when I was a minister is the preaching. I think it's because it's the only part of the role where I ever felt competent. It's taken me many years to get to the point where I feel comfortable acknowledging that I am a good preacher. My reluctance to do so came from a combination of insecurity and that common Protestant brand of pride – false humility. I know now that if God has made you good at something, pretending that you're not very good at it is just extremely disrespectful.

I preached my first sermon on Boxing Day 1993. I was just short of my 17th birthday and had been a Christian for about six months. I don't know many churches that would have given someone like me a chance in the pulpit, and I will always be thankful to Peter Idris Taylor for taking that risk. Every now and then, during my A-Level years, I would turn up at some village chapel to preach. The congregations were always kind, because I was something of a novelty. I don't think anyone else in my school was investing their youth in that particular way. What it means is that, as I approach my 40th birthday, I have had nearly 25 years of preaching experience. That's very helpful, because sometimes it can take you that long to figure out what, how and why you should be preaching what you're preaching.

At some point I will probably share some of my thoughts on the art of preaching, probably on this very blog. Preaching is an art, and a responsibility. Those of us who are doing it should take the development of our skills seriously. I have very high standards for preachers, I'm afraid, but that's OK. Now that I've finally managed to divest myself of false humility it frees me up to start working on developing the real deal.

Growing Old

05 May 2016

"It is the dreadful lie of our culture that you must take the great adventures while you are young. Maybe so in abseiling and Bungee Jumping; but it is not so in the truly dangerous business of the Kingdom."

Peter Volkofsky

It's definitely true that our culture lionises youth. Getting old is seen as a backwards step; a decline; a curse rather than a blessing. But if you're bemoaning your lost youth then you've done nothing more than bought into another lie. There's a Native American saying: "No wise person ever wanted to be younger." The truth is that if you're living well, then you'll be growing in character and wisdom. If you're giving your relationship with God the attention that it deserves then you are more like Christ today than you were this time last year. If this is the case, then you're actually *more* useful to God now than you used to be, and you'll become even more useful the older that you get. The Bible is full of elderly heroes, men and women who didn't hit their stride until the years of experience had caught up with them, and the wisdom of suffering had tempered and focused their youthful energy. Jesus himself spent his youth preparing for the tasks of middle-age. Let me add this: if you aren't nurturing your relationship with God then you've got bigger problems than aching muscles, saggy skin and unwanted hair.

Be encouraged. The world may tell you that your glory days are behind you, that your purpose now is to grow old quietly and aim for nothing more than to be a productive member of United Kingdom PLC, but I tell you that God has *plans*.

Five Children

12 May 2016

Ruth and I have five children, which is about six more than four children. It wasn't such a big deal in Australia, where immigration was the only thing that offset the negative growth rate, but in the UK a large family makes life complicated. People react to our situation in a variety of ways. There are those who display shock or pity, and those who respond as though we're breaking some unspoken rule.

It's possible to view children as a burden - as a drain on the resources of the planet. The doctor who helped deliver our fourth took me to one side after the event and suggested that we had enough children now. He told me that our carbon footprint was big enough. He had a point, but the cynical part of me sometimes wonders if what people really mean to say is, "If you don't stop having children I might have to change my habits as a consumer." There are those who view children as a resource, potential or otherwise. If you follow the news you may be aware that China is softening it's one child policy as a result of studies predicting that the country will face a workforce shortage in the future. Children, for me, are neither a burden nor a resource. They are an expression of hope.

If Ruth and I do our job well then we'll contribute five more people to this earth, who will take the best of us and run with it. Hopefully their character and deeds will more than offset their environmental impact. We are now the parents of a teenager and, if my maths is right, we'll have at least one teenager in the house for about the next fifteen years. Teenagers are, generally speaking, hard work to have around, but some days I look at Calvin and feel fit to burst with pride as I see the man that he is becoming. Here's to the next fifteen years.

A Letter from God

19 May 2016

A little while ago, my three-year old daughter told me that she wanted to write a letter to God. I wrote, while she dictated. It wasn't a very long letter, more of a note, concerned primarily with finding out if God owned a) a cat and b) a space hopper. We put the letter in an envelope and that was that. Naturally, being me, I sensed a teaching opportunity, so I decided to write a reply.

Dear Imogen,

Thank you for the letter that you wrote to me. I loved to receive it. I do not have a cat, but I do like cats. I love everything that I made. I do not have a space hopper, but I don't need one at the moment. Perhaps if I do, I could borrow yours? I love you very much & thank you again for your letter.

Love God.

Apart from the dubious theological statement that God likes cats, I thought it would be a nice moment for Imogen. I put it in an envelope, and a couple of days later 'delivered' it. Imogen was fascinated at first, but after I had read God's reply to her she became quite frightened. I believe the correct phrase is 'she freaked out'. My parenting skills leave a lot to be desired.

On reflection, it makes sense. God is very much a part of our family life, so Imogen is aware of Him, but she is only a child after all. She has never seen God, and is not explicitly conscious of Him working in her life. The transition from God being an abstract idea to a concrete reality that could interact and intervene was probably a bit too much for her at that moment. We all have a crisis point where we have to decide whether or not God is *that* real, and I probably brought it on a bit early...

Still, to be able to talk about God and to be willing to talk to Him, but to be surprised and terrified when He decides to talk back? I can understand fear as an initial response, but eventually we have to decide to either walk away or be all in. Hanging around the fringes, still afraid, doesn't help anyone.

Little and Often

26 May 2016

I magine that you own a plot of land. You want to plant something in it, but it's not in great condition. There are weeds that need to be removed and rocks that need to be cleared. It's a big plot of land, so it's a big job.

The good news is that there's no immediate rush – you've got time. Even if you only move one rock or dig up one weed a day then you'll manage it. It might take a while, but you'll get there. On the other hand, it is a big job. It's a bit overwhelming. You can't help but wonder if it's worth it.

A friend of my wife once told her about her grandmother's attitude towards housework – "Little and often."

Good advice for housework, and equally sound when it comes to developing your spiritual life. Little and often is far better than allowing yourself to become paralysed by the size of the task ahead. It takes time and work to nurture the garden of your soul into fertile soil, but not as much time and work as you might think.

Move a rock here, dig up a weed there. A few verses here, a minute of silent reflection there. The only way that you won't clear that land is if you do nothing.

While it was Still Dark...

02 June 2016

Darkness does strange things to the brain. Sometimes, when you wake in the middle of the night, the darkness makes easily manageable problems seem insurmountable. In the darkness, all our fears and worries can sneak up on us unseen. It's even worse for those of us who are blessed with an overactive imagination. But God being God, it doesn't surprise me at all that He does some of His best work in the darkness.

Imagine being there at the start of the world's calendar, surrounded by the rolling chaos of oppressive darkness, and then to hear that first command – "Let there be light." God does some of His best work in the darkness.

One Sunday, Mary carried her grief all the way to the tomb where Jesus was buried and finds the stone rolled away. John tells us that this happened '…while it was still dark'. Mary is there, in the dark, both figuratively and literally, pondering what has happened. I'll tell you what has happened, Mary. While people were asleep, surrounded by the light-smothering night, God was getting on with the business of resurrection. God does some of His best work in the darkness.

Imagine that. God takes the night, which to us spells death and fear and suffering, and makes it scream of life and light and joy. Of course He'd do it that way. Of course He would. Do you not know Him?

Sometimes the lights go out in our lives and you can't see your hand in front of your face. Don't be afraid, because you know what happens in the dark.

Constructive Anger

09 June 2016

"The reasonable man adapts himself to the world; the unreasonable man persists in trying to adapt the world to himself. Therefore all progress depends on the unreasonable man."

George Bernard Shaw.

B
ack in the Dark Old Days my response to most difficulties was to get depressed. Whether it was criticism, bad news, making a mistake, injustice or inclement weather, the consequence was typically depression. One of the most significant changes that came about as a result of having counselling was that, on the whole, I stopped getting depressed and started getting angry instead. That may not sound like an improvement to some of you, but for me it was a breakthrough. One of the worst things about depression is that it robs you of motivation. You aren't happy, but you feel powerless to do anything about it. It's like being paralysed, and then just having to watch as a snake

devours you whole. No-one says, "I'm feeling depressed today. I'd better change the world."

Anger, on the other hand, at least, has the potential to create significant motivation. In my case, my natural apathy (magnified by the lies of depression) began to burn up in the heat of this new passionate response.

Of course, anger has its own pitfalls. There's a reason why Paul tells us to make sure that our anger doesn't supplant our self-control and result in sin. For me, however, it was much better to learn to channel my anger than it was to try and live with numbing depression. The goal is to keep working at tempering that zeal into a something resembling a godly unreasonableness.

Lighting Fires

16 June 2016

Talking of managing anger, there was once a time when Ruth and I were going through a stressful situation, but we were confident that it would all work out because we had Boris on our side. Boris (not his real name) had said that he'd make sure that everything was sorted out. There was a problem though – namely that Boris wasn't following up on this, and he wasn't delivering on what had been promised. I was feeling let down, anxious and quite angry about it all. Then one morning, as I was waking up and before I'd had the chance to erect my defences for the day, a thought sneaked into my head, like the last sentence of a dream. "You're putting your trust in Boris rather than in Me." I tell you, it's really something to start your day with a divine slap across the wrist.

It's easy to talk of 'trusting God' when the bank account is full, no-one is sick and England haven't yet been knocked out of the tournament, but the reality is that, when these unconscious supports erode, many of us find our 'trust in God' evaporating in the face of panic. It turns out that our trust wasn't really in God in the first place, but rather in our own resources, in our savings, in our clever plans or in Boris.

Larry Crabb, in his excellent book *Connecting*, calls this 'Fire Lighting'.

Who among you fears the Lord
  and obeys the word of his servant?
Let the one who walks in the dark,
  who has no light,
trust in the name of the Lord
  and rely on their God.
But now, all you who light fires
  and provide yourselves with flaming torches,
go, walk in the light of your fires
  and of the torches you have set ablaze.
This is what you shall receive from my hand:
  You will lie down in torment.

  Isaiah 50:10-11

Crabb suggests that the only cure for this malady is a period of intense darkness where we have no choice but to reach out into the black and take God's hand. Then we come to learn that He is the only one worth putting our trust in. Painful lessons are best learnt once.

Why I Am Not Successful

23 June 2016

I f you've read my blog/heard me preach/seen my book, you are by now no doubt saying to yourself, "Wow! This guy is AMAZING! Why is he not a world-famous blogger/preacher/author who is, quite rightly and correctly, making an absolutely fortune from his work?" The truth is that I have no-one to blame but myself. When I was a young man I remember hearing a quote from Martyn Lloyd-Jones – "The worst thing that can happen to a man is for him to succeed before he is ready". Even though I am foolish, I saw that there was wisdom in those words and, as such, one of my prayers over the years has been "Lord, don't let me succeed before I am ready." Funnily enough, God's been 100% on board with that prayer.

Success, as most people perceive it, is actually a wolf in sheep's clothing. It promises much, but behind that sharp-toothed grin is a monster that will destroy you if you are not strong enough to tame it. By contrast, failure can be the making of us, even though we do all we can to keep it at arm's length. Few things test the strength of our foundations like good old fashioned failure, and few things are better for us than when all the stuff that we've built is knocked down so that God can start His own Great Project.

But no-one wants to fail at everything that they do, and neither should we. The issue is really how we define success and what it looks like in a framework of faith. The wise among us already know the truth. The story goes that Mother Teresa was once asked how she measured the success of her work. Her response was, apparently, to look puzzled and then say, "I don't remember that the Lord ever spoke of success. He spoke only of faithfulness in love. This is the only success that really counts."

The Politics of Fear

30 June 2016

I've been thinking a little bit about fear recently. I don't really want to write about Britain's decision to leave the EU, but I feel like I should at least say something. It's too big to ignore; it's too massive to just carry on and pretend it hasn't happened. I'd rather write something else, some spiritual reflection or humourous observation, (like the fact that my spell-checker lets me write 'humour' but wants me to write 'humorous'). But, as I said, I've been thinking about fear recently.

The referendum debate revolved around fear. Fear of economic uncertainty, fear of immigration, fear of eroded sovereignty, fear of the future. Fear seems to be the only tool that our politicians have, and if that's the case – regardless of the referendum result – we're in trouble.

There's no doubt. Fear is a powerful motivator. You can make people do outrageous things, things totally against their character, if you can just make them afraid enough. Yet when I read through the gospels, I can't help but notice that Jesus never seemed to act out of fear. I never get the impression that fear was a factor in his motivation. He did some pretty crazy stuff and upset some powerful people, but he never seemed to be afraid, and if he was then he never let it control his choices.

There was a time when fear came out to play, and that was in the garden of Gethsemane, where he pleads for a different route. He doesn't want to die, especially not like this, and he asks God to spare him. And yet..."Not my will, Father, but yours." Even in his darkest hour, his greatest fear is not death or suffering, but rather the fear of not being obedient.

Imagine living a life where that's really the only thing that you are truly afraid of.

I find it hard to feel optimistic about the immediate future right now. There's all kinds of ugliness and uncertainty surfacing in the Island of the Mighty, but I have decided to not be afraid. Whatever the future brings and whatever actions I take, I will try to not let fear be the thing that drives me. Not my will, Father, but yours.

"Hello?"

07 July 2016

Once upon a time a well-known author and speaker came and spoke at a Christian Union event. The speaker would say something profound, and then end his sentence with something like "Amen?" or "Hello?" It was obvious that he wanted some kind of response, something like "Preach it brother!" or "Hallelujah!" Unfortunately we were the wrong audience. We were a mostly white, mostly middle-to-upper class group of mostly students, some of whom came from fairly conservative church backgrounds. All the speaker got from us was silence. Not one to take defeat lying down, he persevered in an attempt to mould us into his own image. Eventually we got the message that we weren't fulfilling our end of the social contract, so some of us played along a little bit, but you could tell that our hearts weren't in it. It was serious business to him though, and after one of his little pearls of wisdom was met with unsatisfactory enthusiasm he said, "Not many believers here tonight, are there?" What did he mean? That you weren't a Christian if you didn't vocally agree with him? I was not impressed with this encounter. The whole experience just left me cold. I wonder if he knows how arrogant he came across that evening?

I'm not sure that he would care. He didn't strike me as someone who was particularly approachable or open to what anyone else thought. He just struck me as arrogant. Arrogant and humourless.

I have a saying: Never trust a Christian who can't laugh at himself.

Amen?

Alternative Beatitudes

14 July 2016

Blessed are those who have realised that getting bigger and better stuff doesn't lead to happiness, for theirs is the kingdom of heaven.

Blessed are those who, when they see what's on Facebook or listen to the lyrics of the latest chart hit, get depressed, for they will be comforted.

Blessed are those who do more than take Selfies and worry about how many subscribers they have, for they will inherit the earth.

Blessed are those who walk down the high street, find themselves surrounded by materialism and soft porn, and feel empty inside, for they will be filled.

Blessed are those who use technology to build something good, rather than to just make life more convenient, for they will be shown mercy.

Blessed are those who aren't subscribed to Netflix, Amazon Prime or Now TV,
    for they will see God.

Blessed are those who don't get drawn into petty squabbles on Internet forums or YouTube comments,
    for they will be called children of God.

Blessed are those who are mocked and ridiculed and labelled intolerant because they believe in something bigger than what can be seen,
    for theirs is the kingdom of heaven.

Chicken and Egg

21 July 2016

Evangelical Christians don't have a Pope, nor believe in papal infallibility, but sometimes you wouldn't know it from the way that some of us talk about Martin Luther, or John Calvin or our favourite authors or a particular leader or church. It's par for the course for us human beings. We struggle to hold conflicting things in tension; we seek order and patterns in everything, even when there are none. We are happiest when something is clearly 100% good or 100% bad, black or white, right or wrong; we are happiest when our heroes and villains are undiluted. When we're young, and we lack experience, wisdom and courage it's easiest for us if we can attach ourselves to someone and let them do our thinking for us. We all have this subconscious desire to be discipled by something. For some of us, we buy wholeheartedly into a church and adopt uncritically its interpretation of the Bible on faith, love, sex, prayer and God.

I remember once I was doing some teaching to some visitors at Cornerstone. One of the people listening found something I had said difficult to accept in light of what he had been taught by his church and, to his credit, he came to talk to me about it. I took him through one of the New Testament letters which had been influential in shaping my thinking about the topic. I could see, as we went through the letter together, that he wasn't convinced. His knew and respected his church leaders, and who was this nobody trying to tell him that they were wrong? At one point in the letter we came across a verse that, to be honest, may as well have said, "That thing that James is telling you? Yeah, it's right, and that means that what your church has taught you is wrong." He looked at me and said, without a single drop of irony in his voice, "So I just need to find a way to interpret that verse." That was when I knew that I'd lost.

I'd seen it before, in victims of cults. You present an alternative interpretation. It shakes their worldview a little and makes them uncomfortable, so instead of unravelling the thought, exploring it and seeing where it takes them, they run to a church leader who performs some complicated exegetical gymnastics in order to be able to say, "That verse that says that thing – it actually means the complete opposite." And all is right with the world again.

I see it in myself and in others, where instead of letting what the Bible says shape our theology, we let our theology shape what the Bible says. A sad day, when truth knocks on our door, and we just hang out a 'Do Not Disturb' sign.

JAMES WEBB

Thin Places

28 July 2016

I believe in Thin Places. I have two favourites. One is old and one is new. One is inside and one is outside. One is here and one is there.

Canterbury Cathedral is old, at least in terms of this country and its identity. It's been rebuilt several times over the years, but for nearly one and half millennia it has been a site set apart for the service and worship of God. As you wander around it, you can be thinking about the excesses of the established church, the corruption and insipidity of the Anglican faith at its worst, but why should you not be awed by this building? By the size and the beauty. By the devotion that its construction required (The idea that God cannot be glorified by good old fashioned ingenuity and hard work is nonsense by the way). Even in this enlightened day and age, hundreds of visitors are daily looking at stained glass windows and reading Renaissance graffiti. There is something special here. Fifteen hundred years of prayer and song and liturgy? That has to leave a mark.

I will stroll down into the crypt and amble to the Altars of St. Nicholas and St. Mary Magdalene. I may pause to look at the prayers that people have written to be placed on the altar. I will sit and look at the window that shows the harlot drying Jesus' feet with her hair. Even though there may be tourists, I can be silent and listen. I can meet with God. Fifteen hundred years of prayer and song and liturgy, and I add mine to become part of something greater than myself. A blink of the eye for God, but an eternity of praise.

The second place is on the other side of the world. On a small farm on the Belubula, in a place called Canowindra. Many of you won't have heard of it, or of a missionary couple named Ian and Irene, who gave part of their farmland over to Cornerstone. Over forty years ago they planted a grove of poplar trees on that farm. I believe that the plan was for the trees to be sold for matchsticks. That was the plan, but those trees are still there, dead and dangerous, and still very flammable. But that grove has seen more than twenty years of prayer and worship and weddings. I have been involved in all three. Australia is a beautiful country, yet so alien compared to England's green and pleasant fields, and I have sat in the silence of that grove on many a summer morning. I have shed tears and sang songs. I have sat with kangaroos and sheep and birds. I have heard God in some very specific ways, and He and I have wrestled in that place many times. He usually won, but not always.

Thin Places, the Celts called them. Places where the boundary between this life and the next is worn and frail and the freshness of the Kingdom bleeds obviously into the mundane beauty of this world. These places are real, and so is the God who can be found in them.

Tell the Galatians that School's Out

04 August 2016

I wrote this little verse a while ago. It's inspired by Galatians 3:23 to 4:7. Read the passage first.

The law is done?

The pedagogue is agog.

The school uniform doesn't fit any more,

Lay it aside.

Put on the clothes of a son; a daughter,

The attire of a child about your Father's business,

You have come of age.

Get out from behind the nanny's skirt.

Don't go back to the playground,

The classroom.

School's out.

You've been given a fantastic inheritance,

Get out there and claim it.

Walking with God Again

11 August 2016

I was out on one of my walks one evening, and I saw something unusual. Down below me, in her front garden, was an elderly woman, wrapped up against the cold, standing behind a lawn mower. It was a strange sight, seeing this tiny old lady about to start mowing her front lawn in the autumn twilight.

I almost kept walking, but I knew what I had to do.

"Do you need some help?" I yelled down to her.

She didn't hear me. In for a penny, in for a pound. I walked down her steps, got her attention and walked across her lawn until I was standing next to her.

"Do you want me to mow your lawn?" I asked.

It wasn't a big lawn. It wouldn't have taken me long. I explained that I lived just down the road, and that I was often out and about for a walk this time of evening.

At first the lady responded warmly, and made comments about how kind it was of me to offer, but as the conversation went on, something changed. I recognised it. From somewhere, an element of fear had snuck into her mind. In a way I don't blame her. It was probably intimidating, to have this ugly stranger appear out of the darkness and offer to mow her lawn for her. I mean, who does that? Perhaps she thought that I would want to be paid? I don't know. The conversation went politely, but she said that she didn't need my help. Never mind. I had done what was expected of me, and that's all.

I walked on, a mix of conflicting emotions inside. There was the mild embarrassment that comes from having a gift rejected, coupled with the instant self-criticism that told me that it was all my fault. Those were quite easily banished, and then I was just left with sadness as I reflected on how easily we reject the outstretched hand of God because we've allowed the Enemy to whisper lies of fear into our hearts.

On my way back, in the darkness, I saw that the lawn had been freshly mowed and the old lady was nowhere to be seen. This is the kind of thing that happens when you go walking with God.

A Guest Blog from Rev. Ulysses Giblet

18 August 2016

I've been told that every good blog needs a guest blogger now and then. Fortunately, I've been able to convince a long-time friend, the Reverend Ulysses Giblet, to contribute to my page. Here's some of his thoughts on preaching.

When James asked me if I'd write something for his blog, I was happy to help. I decided I should write a short article on a topic that James knows nothing about – preaching.

<u>Why Church Leaders Need to Be Good Preachers:</u>

There are many qualities that are desirable in church leaders, such as punctuality, good personal hygiene and great hair & teeth, but the most important quality for a church leader is the ability to crank out top quality sermons on demand. Here are three reasons why this is the case:

1. *A good Sunday will make people forget about what you did on Monday to Saturday.*

We've all had a bad week at some time. Perhaps we chose our words poorly during a difficult church meeting. Maybe we punched someone in the face during a complicated pastoral situation. What if people are asking tricky questions about why that money from the building fund is resting in your personal bank account? We've all been there – I know that I have. Thankfully, when you're a good preacher, Sunday morning becomes an opportunity to remind people why they employed you. If you can milk a few tears out of the congregation when preaching then they'll be more than happy to overlook your minor failings, such as being unapproachable, pastorally insensitive and morally bankrupt.

2. *Cha Ching!*

If you're anything like me, then you went into the ministry because it involves no heavy lifting and presents fantastic money making opportunities for the right people. If you want to make the big bucks you need to find your way into one of the top tier churches – you know, those mega churches where the congregation is big enough to comfortably employ fifteen full-time members of staff. Some churches also have such distinguished historic reputations that they're full of rich people (who love all that stuff). All the best (i.e. richest) churches have one thing in common – they love excellent preachers. That's what they're looking for in their ministers, so put a bit of effort into improving your preaching and wait for the lucrative job offers to come rolling in. It's even better in America, where an English accent can be worth as much as an extra $10,000 a year. Money for old rope!

3. You only have to be visible one day a week.

If you're an excellent preacher, in a church with a reputation for excellent preaching, then people are happy for you to 'delegate' most of the work of the church to others while you focus on the truly important job of preparing for Sunday's sermon. In fact, they'll probably *insist* on it. Here's a line that you might want to memorise – "I'm sorry, I can't come and help you with that difficult situation, because Mondays through to Thursdays are my sermon preparation days." Fantastic. As added good news, the more experience you have, the quicker you can prepare sermons. After a while, you'll be done by Monday afternoon and have the rest of your 'sermon preparation' days for important spiritual tasks, like sleeping in, eating chocolate and binge watching TV.

Hopefully you can now see why, if you're in church leadership, developing your preaching ability should be your number one priority.

Rev. Ulysses Giblet.

It's Finished when it's Finished

25 August 2016

I've been working on a short story recently. It's a story based on a scene from a screenplay that I wrote, which in turn was based on a short story that appeared in *The Listening Book*. It's all very confusing.

One of the problems that I have when writing is knowing when something is finished. I imagine that other creators feel the same way. I can keep playing with a story indefinitely, like a cat with a dead mouse. I'll cross out the word 'stalked' and replace it with 'walked', and then I'll swap the order of two sentences. Two weeks later I'll come back to the story and cross out the word 'walked' and replace it with 'ambled', and then I'll put the sentences back in their original order.

I wonder if God went through a similar process when He created the world. Was there a first draft where the sun was red and the grass was blue? A second draft where men didn't have nipples? A third draft where He put the nipples back? But it's finished when God declares that "...it is good."

I know people who reject good things on the basis that they aren't perfect. I think that the Church gets unfairly hammered with this a lot. Because someone somewhere did something bad in Jesus' name, it justifies throwing out the baby with the bathwater. Perhaps it's just an excuse really; it's a way of being able to dismiss something that you'd prefer to dismiss, while at the same time making it look like you have the moral high ground. But doing something imperfectly is often better than doing nothing. No-one who moans about people doing something while they do nothing ever has the moral high ground. When it comes to writing, and creating and the Church, 'good' can be good enough.

Passion

01 September 2016

Back when I was at university I somehow, *somehow*, ended up as the Prayer Secretary for the Christian Union. You may as well give Mr. Bean the keys to your Porsche.

At that time there was, amongst certain circles, a devout belief that a spiritual awakening akin to the great Welsh Revival was on its way. Our Christian Union leadership believed this, and decided that we should have a weekly prayer meeting to pray specifically for revival in London. This was, as Prayer Secretary, my responsibility, so I duly arranged the meeting and attended as often as I could, despite my characteristic cynicism. It became apparent that the conviction among the leadership that revival was coming was so solid, so *unshakeable*, that turning up to prayer meetings was obviously unnecessary for them. Three was a good turn out. I liked the times when it was just me who showed up, to be honest. It was good for my misanthropic soul.

One day, there was a new face at the prayer meeting. A guy who'd just started at the university. He began by telling me how passionate he was for revival, how he longed for nothing more than to see God do something amazing in the city. I looked at the clock. It was 6:05pm. The meetings would go for anything from half an hour to forty five minutes, and if this guy's enthusiasm was anything to go by this one might be decent after all. But my initial hope was very soon dashed to pieces on dull rocks. We had awkward silence, uninspiring muttered prayers, lots of looking down at your feet in what Adrian Plass calls 'the Shampoo Position'. Pick a random page from the 'Dull Prayer Meeting' play book, we did it. We struggled through for what seemed like half an hour, and then I looked at the clock. It was 6:07pm. Have you ever been in a prayer meeting like that? George Harrison once said, "The Beatles saved the world from boredom." He was wrong.

After the meeting finished, we had a few minutes of awkward chat and went our separate ways. He didn't come to the meeting the following week, or the week after that, or ever again. I didn't blame him, but still, he'd said that he was passionate about revival. Eventually, the prayer meetings fizzled out due to lack of interest. I'm not sure what God thought about it all, but I do know one thing. Talking about how passionate you are doesn't count.

JAMES WEBB

The Wisdom of Old Ladies

08 September 2016

When I was at Spurgeon's, our Pastoral Care lecturer told us that he had spoken to his mother on the phone recently. She had told him that she had gone to an evening fellowship group at someone's house, and when she had arrived, the young assistant minister was already there and had made himself at home in the most comfortable armchair available. "Tell your students not to do that," she told her son. He passed this on to us, not because it had anything to do with pastoral care but because he was just doing what his mum had told him to do. My time at Spurgeon's was very beneficial to me, but as far as practical lessons go, that was one of the few that I can remember. I've always chosen my seat very carefully since. There's wisdom in some of these old ladies.

Rev. Tim Ditchfield was the chaplain at my university. I remember him saying that if you asked him who was the holiest person that he knew, he would have to pick an old lady who had been at the church where he was a student. He said that she didn't have the appearance of holiness, being an old lady who lived in a block of flats and smoked like a chimney, but she and God had an understanding. He told a fantastic story to back this up. I'm not 100% sure of some of the unimportant details, but it's too good a story to not share.

Coincidentally, this is also a fellowship group armchair story. They were meeting at this old lady's flat and the group was one chair short this particular evening. Tim offered to sit on the floor, but the old lady wouldn't hear of it. "Let's pray about it," she said. She then proceeded to lead the group in a prayer that went something like this: "God, you know we need another chair for this meeting, so please provide one. Oh, and make it a green one, because green is my favourite colour." She then said to Tim, "You'd better go and get this chair then."

Tim left the flat and wandered up and down the corridor outside totally at a loss as to what to do. What a crazy situation to find yourself in. Then just as he was passing the lift he heard a *ping*. He watched as the doors slid open. The lift was empty, except for a single green armchair.

Some of those dear old ladies are *dangerous*.

Gam Zeh Ya'Avor

15 September 2016

Life has its own rhythms. There are creatively fruitful times, where the inspiration flows; there are times where I feel jaded and uninspired. There doesn't always seem to be any reason for the transition. Sometimes, it's just suddenly different. A couple of weeks ago, I had ideas. This week, I don't have any, and the ones I had a couple of weeks ago sit there on my desk like paperweights. What to do when it feels like you'll never have a good idea again?

One thing I've found helpful is this apocryphal story. It exists in many forms throughout the world, but this is one version:

Benaiah Ben Yehoyada was King Solomon's most trusted advisor, but the King thought he needed a lesson in humility, so he set him an impossible task. He asked Benaiah to find him a specific ring in time for Sukkot, which was six months away.

"The ring I've heard of," said Solomon, "has magical powers. A happy man who looks at it becomes sad, while a sad man becomes happy. Find me this ring."

Benaiah left to search for the ring but could not find it, for no such ring existed. The day before Sukkot he wandered through a poor district in Jerusalem, distraught. He passed a jewellers shop, and in desperation went in to ask the jeweller if he had ever heard of such a ring. The jeweller smiles, produces a plain gold band and engraves something on it. He then passes it to Benaiah, who reads the inscription and smiles.

The following day, Benaiah presented the ring to his King, and when Solomon read the inscription it was he that was humbled.

The Hebrew inscription read *gam zeh ya'avor*, which means 'This too shall pass'.

Standing on the Shoulders of Giants

22 September 2016

I was discussing with someone who suggested that, as an atheist, he at least was '…thinking for himself'. I pointed out that, unless he had invented atheism, he actually wasn't. None of us really think for ourselves, I told him. There are thousands of years of history and debate and experience behind each of us, and all we can ever do is just pick a side.

I don't think that there are any truly original thoughts left. We're all just building on what's gone before and I try to be open about this. I am very happy to name and shame those who have influenced me. The truth is that everything that I write on this blog, even the really good stuff, has had its origins – at least – in something given to me by others. Even the conclusions that I have arrived at on my own have been built on foundations laid by books I have read and people I have known. The other day I jotted down some thoughts on the internal conflict between good and evil, but those thoughts came to me while I was reflecting on what I had been reading in *Connected* by Larry Crabb. My earlier posts about the Parable of the Talents were my own thoughts on the subject, but it was people in Cornerstone who got me thinking in that direction.

This is exactly how God intended it to be. No man is an island, wrote John Donne; as human beings we do nothing and go nowhere without others around us. There's no discipline on the planet, whether it's music, sport, writing, medicine or anything, where you can become an expert by distancing yourself from its community. You can't withdraw from the world and then teach yourself brain surgery (well, you can, but probably only once). You can't get better at something without knowing what's worked and what hasn't worked before. Growth does not occur without interdependence. In the same way, we will never become expert disciples by rejecting the community of believers, whether that's our local Christian community, the global Church or the Communion of Saints in whose footsteps we tread.

Be patient, watch and learn, and then go and build something grand on the foundations of those who have gone before.

Newsworthy

29 September 2016

A friend of mine once told me about a small group of young people from his church that had gone and done some praiseworthy good deed. Local television sent a news crew to ask what had motivated them to do such a noble thing. Most of the group gave safe answers, but one girl talked about how her actions were an expression of her faith in Christ. I'll let you guess which was the one piece of footage that they didn't use when they ran the story.

We get used to Christianity being on the receiving end of selective reporting. The Christian faith usually features only when it's held up as an ugly or bland contrast to some other more noteworthy hot topic, like homosexuality or Islam or Richard Dawkins. Sometimes we feel so victimised that we get excited when we finally see a media report that champions 'Christian values', crying "See! Someone important agrees with us!" as we share it with all our Facebook friends.

Michael Banner, my ethics lecturer at King's, said something on this topic. When you see such an article, he said, don't get carried away; they are most certainly not running that piece because they have a Christ-centred world-view. What they are championing are the idols of 'Family Values' or 'Traditional Morality'. That's not the same as Christian. In fact, Christ is in opposition to anything that merely has the appearance of true religion. Don't be fooled into thinking that this journalist is on your side, and be very cautious about aligning yourself with him.

When Cornerstone was out in Bourke they were heavily involved in the local community. When you get a group of talented people with a desire to make this Christianity thing work, then it should be no surprise that they go around meeting needs where they can. However, a national paper once ran a piece in their weekend magazine about this suspicious Christian cult that was taking over an outback town. Imagine if your church was heavily involved in good work in the community and then, out of nowhere, a national news outlet runs a piece basically saying, "Ah yes, but what's their real motivation?" This idea of Cornerstone as some Machiavellian consortium out to build its own little Caliphate is a far cry from my own experience. Not everything you read in the paper reflects reality.

When I spoke to Paul Roe about that article he didn't seem too bothered, in fact, he seemed quite pleased. His view was that if the atheists are being kept awake at night worrying about what you're up to, then you're probably on the right track. When you look at the stories spread about Christ by those who held the media power of the day, then you have to admit that he's got a point. If you take the teachings of Jesus seriously, and dare to bring them with you out of the private sphere into the public, then you shouldn't be surprised if the papers run front page spreads warning people of your dangerous, subversive behaviour or crowing over your mistakes. As Richard Wurmbrand wrote, "If you choose to walk the way of oneness with God, men will blow trumpets at your every misstep. Do not wonder! In this world, the wind is always in Christ's face. The world agrees with true religion only in the measure to which God agrees with the devil."

I have a quote on my wall that, as an inveterate people pleaser, I know I need to take to heart. It's something that Jesus said:

"Woe to you when all men speak well of you, for that is how their fathers treated the false prophets."

Self Pity and Lolly-Sticks

06 October 2016

L ike all the best people, I'm prone to self-pity. "Why me...?" I might say, or maybe "Everyone else has it better than me..." or "They never have problems, unlike me..." and sometimes "Why can't I just get a break?" etc. It feels quite good, but it's really just a way of saying, "Life isn't treating me the way that I'm entitled to be treated", and as such self-pity is nothing more than cleverly disguised pride. Well, for me, at least. I'm sure that for you your whining is entirely justified.

One of the best ways of knocking the self-pity goblin on the head is thankfulness. I've already written about the importance of gratitude, but the great thing about being thankful is that it has real-life, goblin-killing, magical powers!

One of my children attended an after-school club called *Pilgrimz*. No, that's not a typo; apparently that's the kind of thing that appeals to The Youf these days. *Pilgrimz* is a Christian group, run by one of the local clergy and helpers. It follows the tried-and-tested formula of Bible story and craft activity (One day I'll write an entire blog post on why this is such an excellent combination). After one particular session Xanthe brought home a pot filled with old ice-lolly sticks. On the sticks she had written the names of family and friends. She was supposed to draw a stick at random and do something kind for the person named on the stick. Now that's not a bad idea.

Anyway, it gave me an idea, and now I commend it to you. On my desk I have a 'Best Dad Ever' mug that was given to me as a Father's Day present. In that mug are a bundle of coloured lolly-sticks. On each stick I've written the name of a person, or a church, or an organisation, or I might have written a word or two that relates to a particular thing I've learnt or experienced – sometimes an enjoyable thing, sometimes a painful thing, but always something that has left me better off than I was before. When the self-pity goblin knocks at the door, I draw a stick at random and spend just a couple of seconds thanking God for the name or experience written on the stick. Maybe I'll draw a second, or a third, or a fourth stick. Maybe I won't. It doesn't really matter, because one tends to do the job. I'll tell you this, I have never found anything that kills self-pity quicker than my cup of lolly-sticks.

Going Back

13 October 2016

> *They said, "Is this not Jesus, the son of Joseph, whose*
> *father and mother we know? How can he now say, 'I came*
> *down from heaven'?"*

> *John 6:42*

I'm not one who enjoys change, but I do quite like new beginnings. One of the best things about going to university was being able to leave the past behind. No longer would I be defined by my school's social hierarchy – I could reinvent myself and start all over again!

But when you've moved away, it can be hard going back. When I return to an old church to preach I wonder how many people are actually listening to my sermon, and how many are dwelling on the mistakes I made fifteen years ago, or thinking "Ah, there's James. He's one of ours. What a lovely boy. I remember when he sang *Walking in the Air* to raise money for charity. Hilarious." After all, how can you take a preacher seriously as a harbinger of God when you have warm fuzzy memories of him as an awkward sixteen-year old sweating through his first ever sermon?

Even though Canterbury is a new place for me, Ruth's family has lived here for a long time. When we first arrived it was odd to meet people that I didn't know, but who already seemed to know bits and pieces about me because of the news that had, quite understandably, trickled down the family grapevine. Sometimes your hopes for a fresh beginning are shipwrecked from the start.

People change, hopefully for the better, and sometimes in a very short space of time. We don't do anyone a favour by assuming that they're still the person that they were ten years ago and treating them as such. One of the kindest things you can do for someone else is to leave plenty of room in your head for them to grow.

Not Easy

20 October 2016

He doesn't make it easy for us. In John 10 you can read about a group who came to Jesus to ask him a question.

"Are you the Messiah, Jesus? Give us a straight answer. No games now. Yes or no. Are you the one?"

"I'm not giving you anything else, " said Jesus. "I've said my piece and done what I'm going to do. The ball's in your court. What are *you* going to do?"

How easy it would be if we all awoke tomorrow morning to see YES, I DO EXIST scorched across the sky in flame. How easy it would be if, in a coordinated effort, flag-waving angels appeared on motorways across the world. How easy it would be. Instead we find ourselves in a staring contest with God, but rather than submitting we stubbornly dare the creator to blink first.

There was no sign of the risen Jesus in Herod's palace on that Sunday morning. He didn't walk those halls, waving to the startled servants with a nail-scarred hand. Neither did he appear to Pilate during breakfast, disturbing him in his meal in order to say, "I told you so."

Instead he appears only to the terrified, uncertain, defeated mob of those who had already thrown their lot in with him. A perfect moment to prove to the unbelievers that he had been right, but instead he wastes it by showing himself only to those who were already on his side.

"I'll follow you Jesus. I'll do what you want, but…well, I need a little more proof. It's a big decision, isn't it? I have to be sure."

"I'm not giving you anything else," says Jesus. "I've said my piece and done what I'm going to do. The ball's in your court. What are *you* going to do?"

No wonder he said, "Blessed are those who believe without having to see."

But He doesn't make it easy for us.

Annual Review

27 October 2016

This post marks the first year anniversary of *The Listening Book* blog. I've been scribbling on this page once a week for a whole year now. It would be a good time to stop and reflect on what's happened over the past twelve months, but I'm not going to do that. "What has happened in the past year?" is a good question, but a more important one is "Am I a better man than I was this time last year?"

Life is anything but predictable, and for many of us it can seem like a riding a roller-coaster with the lights out. We have no idea what's coming next, we're just hanging on for dear life. Judging whether or not you've had a good year based on whether or not good things have happened to you is a recipe for disappointment. You're surrendering your mental well-being to things that you can't control. But being a disciple is something you do have control over, so why not judge your year based on that? A good year is any year in which you have grown as a follower of Jesus, regardless of what circumstance has brought your way. If you hold on to that, then every year can be a good year.

Ask yourself this: "Am I growing?"

If the answer is "Yes" then all is right with the world.

ABOUT THE AUTHOR

James is a writer, a father, a husband, a follower of Jesus and a lover of board games, though not necessarily in that order. Sometimes he even manages to do some of these things quite well. He's crammed quite a lot of experiences into his life so far, such as working for Tearfund; being a Baptist minister; living in Australia as part of a mission & discipleship community and watching QPR beat Oldham Athletic at Loftus Road on the 27th December 1993. It's not been all bad.

The Ramblings of the Man Who Bought a Pear is his third published book. If you were compiling a list of the best books that he has written, this one would definitely be in the top three.

He and his family currently live in Canterbury, England.

JAMES WEBB

BOOKS BY THE SAME AUTHOR

The Listening Book: The Soul Painting & Other Stories

This is a beautiful book, in words and images, and will appeal to old and young and all those in between. As the title suggests, the stories are perfect for reading aloud and could be used in a range of settings. The delicate images add another dimension. From fables to folk tales, from stories told around the camp fire to John Lewis Christmas ads, humankind responds to the power of story and to the meaning that narratives give us.
Sophie Duffy
Author of *Bright Stars*, *The Generation Game* and *This Holey Life*.

Job 28 pictures the search for wisdom as digging for gold. The Listening Book has numerous nuggets to mine, embedded in stories that will help you to remember them.
Steve Divall
Senior Pastor, St Helen's Church, North Kensington.

Hardback ISBN: 978-0-9934383-0-1   Softback ISBN: 978-0-9934383-2-5
EBook ISBN: 978-0-9934383-1-8 Audiobook via Amazon/Audible
Religion: Inspirational
Lioness Writing Ltd Release date: 31 October 2015
144 pages, 8.5 inches x 8.5 inches, 25 colour photographs and 3 B&W photos

The Second Listening Book: Loaded Question & Other Stories

I enjoy reading James Webb, not just because he is a gifted and imaginative storyteller, but because he provides nourishing soul food for the journeys we all make through the deserts of life. With his creative imagination he provokes a range of emotions in the reader and I invite you to step inside and be prepared to find something for which your soul has cried out.

David Coffey OBE
Global Ambassador for BMS World Mission.

There are very few books I read that can make me laugh and think profoundly at the same time. This book however is one of them. As a child I used to watch Tales of the Unexpected and loved the twists at the end - James' book easily surpasses them. It is very easy to read and yet worthwhile at the same time as each story contains spiritual truths (which aren't at all preachy and sometimes not obvious!). This is a book you have to try - you won't regret it.

Eric Harmer
Pastor of Barton Church, Canterbury and Author of
Build-Your-Own Bible Study.

Hardback ISBN: 978-0-9934383-6-3   Softback ISBN: 978-0-9934383-4-9
EBook ISBN: 978-0-9934383-7-0 Audiobook via Amazon/Audible
Religion: Inspirational
Lioness Writing Ltd Release date: 31 October 2016
158 pages, 8.5 inches x 8.5 inches, 31 black & white illustrations and photos

MORE POSTS

www.thelisteningbook.org.uk

You can contact James at

author@thelisteningbook.org.uk